Hg2 Berlin

A Hedonist's guide to
Berlin

BY Sarah Marshall
PHOTOGRAPHY Sarah Marshall

A Hedonist's guide to Berlin

Managing director – Tremayne Carew Pole
Marketing director – Sara Townsend
Series editor – Catherine Blake
Design – P&M Design
Maps – Richard Hale
Typesetting – Dorchester Typesetting
Repro – PDQ Digital Media Solutions Ltd
Printer – Printed in Italy by Printer Trento srl
Publisher – Filmer Ltd

Email – info@ahedonistsguideto.com
Website – www.ahedonistsguideto.com

First published in the United Kingdom in June 2005 by
Filmer Ltd
47 Filmer Road
London SW6 7JJ

ISBN – 0-9547878-7-0

Hg2 Berlin

CONTENTS

How to…

A Hedonist's guide to… is broken down into easy to use sections:
Sleep, Eat, Drink, Snack, Party, Culture, Shop, Play and Info. In each of
these sections you will find detailed reviews and photographs.

At the front of the book you will find an introduction to the city and
an overview map, followed by descriptions to the four main areas and
more detailed maps. On each of these maps you will see the places
that we have reviewed, laid out by section, highlighted on the map with
a symbol and a number. To find out about a particular place, simply
turn to the relevant section, where all entries are listed alphabetically.

Alternatively, browse through a specific section (i.e. Eat) until you find
a restaurant that you like the look of. Next to your choice will be a
small coloured dot – each colour refers to a particular area of the city
– then simply turn to the relevant map to discover the location.

Updates

Due to the lengthy publishing process and shelf lives of books it is
very difficult to keep travel guides up to date – new restaurants, bars
and hotels open up all the time, while others simply fade away or just
go out of style. What we can offer you are free updates – simply log
onto our website www.ahedonistsguideto.com or www.hg2.net and
enter your details, answer a relevant question to provide proof of purchase and you will be entitled to free updates for a year from the date
that you sign up. This will enable you to have all the relevant information at your fingertips whenever you go away.

In order to help us, if you have any comments or recommendations
that you would like to see in the guide in future please feel free to
email us at info@ahedonistsguideto.com.

The concept

A Hedonist's guide to... is designed to appeal to a more urbane and stylish traveller. The kind of traveller who is interested in gourmet food, elegant hotels and seriously chic bars – the traveller who feels the need to explore, shop and pamper themselves away from the madding crowd.

Our aim is to give you the inside knowledge of the city, to make you feel like a well-heeled, sophisticated local and to take you to the most fashionable places in town to rub shoulders with the local glitterati.

In today's world work rules our life, weekends away are few and far between, and when we do go away we want to have the most fun and relaxation possible with the minimum of stress. This guide is all about maximizing time. Everywhere is photographed, so before you go you know exactly what you are getting into; choose a restaurant or bar that suits you and your demands.

We pride ourselves on our independence and our integrity. We eat in all the restaurants, drink in all the bars and go wild in the nightclubs – all totally incognito. We charge no one for the privilege of appearing in the guide; every place is reviewed and included at our discretion.

We feel cities are best enjoyed by soaking up the atmosphere and the vibrancy; wander the streets, indulge in some retail relaxation therapy, re-energize yourself with a massage and then get ready to eat like a king and party hard on the stylish local scene.

We feel that it is important for you to explore a city on your own terms, while the places reviewed provide definitive coverage in our eyes; one's individuality can never be wholly accounted for. Sometimes if you take that little extra time to wander off our path, then you may just find that truly hidden gem that we missed.

Berlin

It's often hard to imagine Berlin as the capital of Germany. A city of constant uprising, endless innovation and unpredictable change hardly fits the bill as head of a traditionally conservative and straight-laced nation. But Berlin is an island, a glitch in the system, an anomaly on an otherwise meticulously structured landscape.

Much of this can be explained by the city's troubled and tumultuous history. A former capital of Prussia, the Weimar Republic and the Third Reich, Berlin was historically divided in four sectors after World War II. Within a few years it became two halves: the East (known as the GDR) was governed by the Soviets, while the West came under Western Allied rule. The two halves co-existed uncomfortably until 1961 when Erich Honecker authorized the building of a reinforced border almost overnight. This Wall would stand for 28 years, in which time 80 people died trying to cross it.

During this period, Berlin's history became a tale of two cities. And while a decision to reunite the city was met with unanimous praise, the two satellite states would only ever collide awkwardly. Even today, Berlin remains fractured and decentralized. There are two main shopping drags, two key cultural areas and even two kinds of traffic lights. (There have been several nostalgic campaigns to save the 'the little green men of the East'.) Locals prefer to stick within their own *kiez* (area), with its own distinctive identity and character.

Much of the city's focus has, however, shifted eastwards, with Mitte and Prenzlauer Berg a hub of social activity. As dissatisfied

Ossies (East Berliners) fled their homes in 1989, a disaffected Western youth moved in to fill the vacuum. A property free-for-all ensued and Berliners partied hard. Although things have calmed down since, a legacy of hedonism remains. A creative community thrives on low rents and relaxed licensing laws, and a sense of independent innovation prevails. No other city boasts so many clubs, bars, cafés and restaurants in such concentration. Anyone with enough motivation can embark on an

enterprise and there's always room for experiment. While other European capitals have bowed down to corporates, chains such as Starbucks have struggled in Berlin. Notably absent elsewhere, this city has possibility.

Constantly in flux, Berlin never stands still. Venues open and close at the bat of an eyelid, and many prefer to remain hidden from public view. All of this can be frustrating for the visitor. Equally, there's ample opportunity for exploration and discovery. Peer into a quiet courtyard and you'll find a fashion boutique; wander past a disused power station at the right time of night and you'll be dragged into a full-blown party.

In truth, nothing about Berlin really seems to fit. Who'd have thought, for instance, that a landlocked city would have so many man-made beaches? Look beyond the austere architecture and you'll find a city of unquantifiable beauty. Historically, Berlin has defied law and conformity. Today, it defies expectation.

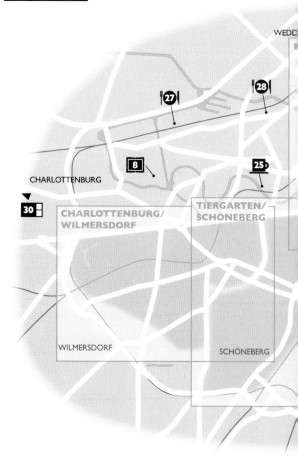

0   1km   2km

WEDD

CHARLOTTENBURG

CHARLOTTENBURG/
WILMERSDORF

TIERGARTEN/
SCHÖNEBERG

WILMERSDORF

SCHÖNEBERG

 SLEEP

30. Schlosshotel im
    Grunewald

 EAT

27. Parc Fermé
28. Paris-Moskau

PRENZLAUER BERG

GESUNDBRUNNEN

PRENZLAUER
BERG

KREUZBERG / FRIEDRICHSHAIN

ALEXANDER-
PLATZ

FISCHERINSEL

FRIEDRICHSHAIN

MITTE

KREUZBERG

8

EDLUNG
TEMPELHOF

25

PARTY

8. Insel
25. Kit Kat Club

CULTURE

8. Schloss Charlottenburg

SNACK

25. Schleusenkrug

Mitte and Prenzlauer Berg

In the past 15 years, the neighbouring districts of Mitte and Prenzlauer Berg have come to represent the emerging face of modern Berlin. When the Wall fell in 1989, the city's social focus quickly shifted towards the East and these two areas became a nucleus for political regeneration and post-Reunification celebrations. As an embittered GDR population fled to greener grass on the other side of the fence, a disaffected West Berlin youth moved in. Houses were left empty with sheets on beds and water still hot in the kettles. Squatters claimed space and the parties started. And they continue – and Berlin's biggest concentration of bars and clubs can be found here. Admittedly many are short-lived, but there's a sense of youthful vibrancy that seems determined never to die.

Geographically Mitte ('middle') lies in the centre of the city; it was the sand islands on this particular stretch of the Spree that initially gave birth to Berlin. As it's the meeting-point between East and West, government buildings, theatres, the opera house and many major museums are all based here. The bourgeois avenues of Friedrichstraße and Unter den Linden (named after the Linden trees that line the grand street) feature elements of Berlin's chequered history, from the Brandenburg Gate and Checkpoint Charlie to the Jewish quarter of Scheunenviertel. The Museuminsel (built in the late 18th century) contains five of the city's most important museums.

The area around Hackescher Markt and Scheunenviertel is characterized by a special type of housing known as '*Hinterhöfe*'. The pedestrian passageways that run through these courtyards are now home to innumerable cafés, galleries and clothes stores – many hidden from the street. Once an area of squats and anarchic activity, gentrification has since taken root in Mitte, which is now a thriving media district. The last remaining squat structures can be found at Tacheles. Dominated by the Fernsehturm (known to locals affectionately as the 'Alex'), Alexanderplatz is a hub of activity and Berlin's entry point for travellers by train. It has also become a symbol for the capital's new eastward-leaning identity.

Cross the graphic design studios and young boutiques of Torstraße to enter the bohemian and peaceful district of Prenzlauer Berg. Unlike Mitte, the tourist industry has yet to make itself felt here – this is East Berlin at its most characteristic. Once a *Grunderzeit* (residential district for the working class), the area is now home to actors, artists and young families. Surprisingly, Prenzlauer Berg has the highest birth rate of any one place in Europe and it's not uncommon to see trendy young mums pushing state-of-the-art pushchairs along the cobbled roads. As it remained largely unscathed by the bombs of World War II, many of its beautiful townhouses remain intact and these pleasant leafy streets are a popular destination for a Sunday stroll.

Known as Berlin's café district, Prenzlauer Berg has a distinctly European feel. The area around Kollwitzplatz and the Wasserturm is particularly popular. Once a meeting-point for drug-dealers, the Helmholzplatz now hosts a high concentration of reputable bars and cafés. Fans of street art should take a look at graffiti pieces on the walls of the community centre – the work of several international artists. Severe fashion statements are made on the ultra-hip Kastanienallee – a street responsible for the image of cool Berlin portrayed in our style press.

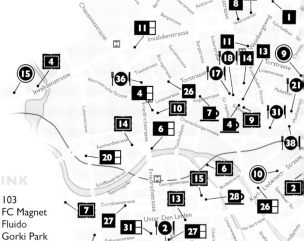

0   0.5   1km

M Metro Station

CULTURE

2.   Berliner Fernsehturm
4.   Hamburger Bahnhof
      Gallery
6.   Pergamon Museum
7.   Reichstag
9.   Sammlung Hoffman
10. Tacheles
13. Staatsoper
14. Berliner Ensemble
15. Maxim Gorki
17. Volksbühne

EAT

2.   Borschardt
11. Gugelhof
14. I Due Forni
17. Kasbah
18. Kuchi
20. Lutter und Wegner
21. Monsieur Vuong
22. Nocti Vagus
24. Oderquelle
25. Offenbach Stuben
26. Oki
29. Pasternak
30. Sasaya
31. Schwarzenraben
35. Vau
36. Weinbar Rutz
37. Zander
38. Zoe

SLEEP

1.   Ackselhaus
2.   Adlon Hotel
4.   Arcotel Velvet
5.   Art'otel Ermelerhaus
6.   Artist Riverside Hotel
8.   Dorint Am
      Gendarmenmarkt
11. The Honigmond
20. Künstlerheim Louise
23. Myers Hotel
26. Radisson SAS
27. The Regent
31. Westin Grand

Charlottenburg and Wilmersdorf

Stepping into West Berlin is like entering another city. In contrast to the transient bar and café scene of the East, Charlottenburg and Wilmersdorf are far more established. The buildings look smarter, the cars more flash and the pace is considerably slower. This is the decadent Berlin famously portrayed by Liza Minelli et al in 'Cabaret' – a million miles from the bleak architecture of the east.

Following Reunification, the city's demographic shifted with Berlin's younger generations migrating east. Initially the change was quite dramatic, but in recent years the flux has stabilized. Club and bar openings are on the increase and the one-time disaffected youth are starting to trickle back home. That said, you'd be hard-pushed to find an East Berliner who'd consider crossing west and vice-versa.

Berlin's busiest shopping district is located along the Ku'damm. The fractured spire of the Kaiser Wilhelm Memorial Church is the area's most notable landmark. A one-time hang-out for junkies and unsavoury characters, the Zoologischer Garten forms a major gateway to the West. It's since been cleaned up, but the neon lights and tourist-trap

eateries are an unforgettable reminder of a seedy past. Travel further along the never-ending street and you'll stumble on some of the

biggest names in fashion design, along with the fantastic KaDeWe – Berlin's answer to Harrods. Berlin's stylish design hotels (Q! and K'udamm 101) are also located in this area.. The road takes its name from the Prussian Kurfürst ('Elector') and was originally just a track leading from the Elector's residence to the Grunewald. In 1886 it was remodelled by Bismark on the grand boulevards of Paris.

Far more pleasant is the area around Savignyplatz, with its innumerable chic boutiques, restaurants and cafés. During the day, it's the reserve of ladies-who-lunch and at night an affluent restaurant crowd descend. A pretty picture of 19th-century buildings line the tranquil streets of Bleibtreustraße, while Berlin's major jazz clubs, concert halls and theatres can also be found nearby (the cabaret and excess of the 1920s had their roots here). Fasanenstraße also has some especially good spots.

Many of Berlin's better restaurants can also be found this side of town. Generally, the quality of food and location is consistently higher. While neighbourhood favourites such as Florian and Lubitsch are popular with locals, try Jules Verne for innovative fusion cuisine and Engelbecken for a lakeside retreat. While operating a safe distance from the cutting egde, both Charlottenburg and Wilmersdorf undeniably represent Berlin's past and present glories.

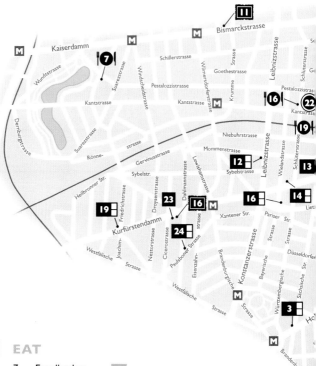

Kreuzberg and Friedrichshain

Although technically part of West Berlin, Kreuzberg is culturally and spiritually more akin to the East, and traditionally an area of militant radicalism – Berlin's May Day riots draw a strong following from this neighbourhood. In the '70s and '80s students famously rallied against city planners' attemps to demolish large areas of housing. The left-wing punk scene, so synonymous with late '80s Berlin, also found a breeding ground in Kreuzberg. Today social unrest has subsided, but the area is still popular with an alternative crowd.

Berlin has a massive Turkish community and is considered the fifth largest Turkish city in the world. Much of the population settled in Kreuzberg, where they were largely left to their own devices. Every Tuesday and Friday an open-air Turkish market takes place along the Landwehrkanal at Paul Linke Ufer. Contrary to popular belief, the donar kebab was actually invented in Berlin and the legacy lives on in the rows of fantastic kebab stores that line the Mehringdam and Skalitzer Strasse. In contrast to other predominantly white suburbs, there's something refreshingly international about Kreuzberg.

The district itself is so sprawling, it's been split in two along the division of the old postal codes. 'Kreuzberg 61' covers the more affluent and conservative streets around the pretty Bergmannstraße. Fortunately, having survived the wartime bombing, many of the cobbled streets and Prussian façades remain. In a city not known for its beauty, this is a truly scenic place. Antique stores, cafés and boutique clothes shops attract visitors by day, but as daylight disappears so too does much of the action. The peaceful Viktoriapark can be found on the 'cross-hill' from which Kreuzberg derives its name. Schinkel's 1821 monument to the Napoleonic Wars lies at the summit, and many nearby streets are named after battles and generals from that period.

An edgier neighbourhood around Schlesisches Tor is known as 'Kreuzberg 36'. This is where most of the nightlife takes place. Lo-fi indie bars and rock venues line the Oranienstraße, while much of the original Kreuzberg community chooses to hang out along Wiener Straße and around Görlitzer Park. A further cycle ride east along the Spree is up-and-coming Treptow – particularly worth a visit in the summer when several riverside bars are open.

The Oberbaumbrücke links Kreuzberg to the neighbouring district of Friedrichshain, and was once a boundary between West and East. During the Cold War, the bridge was used as a border post and spy exchange point. Today, it's the location for an annual water fight between residents of both areas, who share a friendly rivalry. Along with water, combatants have also been known to fire rotten vegetables across the river at the opposition.

The final bastions of squat-living reside in the bohemian and architecturally bleak area of Friedrichshain. To check out authentic squats, take a walk along Rigaer Straße. Hosting a massive student population, it's also one of the cheapest places in Berlin and home to a grotty but vibrant bar scene. A great flea market also takes place every Sunday at Boxhagener Platz. The eerily atmospheric 90-metre wide Karl Marx Allee, meanwhile, provides some fine examples of GDR architecture. Originally built under Stalin's orders as a showpiece between 1952 and 1965, it was known as Stalinallee until 1961. Amid the prefab building blocks, there are some fantastic buildings; both the Kino International and showcase Russian restaurant Café Moskau (see Party) are worth a look. Several bars and restaurants have opened along this stretch and it's currently experiencing a regeneration.

⦿| EAT

1. Abendmahl
3. Brot und Rosen
4. Chez Gino
5. Le Cochon Bourgeois
6. Defne
8. ETA Hoffman
12. HH Müller
15. Jolesch
23. Noi Quattro
32. Spindler & Klatt
34. Svevo
39. Zur Henne

◯ PARTY

2. 103 Club
3. Berghain/Panorama Bar
5. Café Moskau
6. Geburtstagklub
11. Lovelite
13. Maria
14. Pavillon
16. Sage
18. Watergate
20. WMF
21. Yaam@Hoppetosse

⬛ DRINK

4. Bar Nou
6. Club der Visionäre
7. Der Freischwimmer
15. KMA Bar
17. Neue Bohnen
19. Orient Lounge
20. San Remo Upflamör
21. Sanatorium 23
29. Würgeengel
30. Zebrano

0   0.5   1km

Kreuzberg and Friedrichshain local map

CULTURE

3. East Side Gallery
5. Jüdisches Museum
20. Pomp Duck & Circumstance

SNACK

2. Ankerklause
5. Bateau Ivre
6. Café am Engelbeken
12. Café Schönbrunn
15. Cream
16. Ehrenburg
20. Kaffee Am Meer
23. Knofi
24. Morganland
29. Tiki Heart
31. Van Loon
32. Volckswirtschaft

SLEEP

22. Mövenpick Hotel

Schöneberg and Tiergarten

The vast green expanse of Tiergarten separates Mitte and Charlottenburg and, physically at least, explains why these two areas are worlds apart. Stretching west from the Brandenburg Gate, the park has had an interesting history. Initially, it was a 16th-century hunting-ground; wealthy Berliners then chose to reside here and their dwellings were later to become the city's embassy buildings. It was bombed in the War and denuded during the severe winter of 1945–46 when many of the trees were cut down for firewood; since then towns from all over Germany have donated trees to assist in the recovery. All roads entering Tiergarten lead to a 19th-century Prussian Victory Column, which was transferred here from the Reichstag.

The futuristic Potsdamer Platz complex was originally intended as a commercial showpiece to mark Berlin's reunification. After being utterly destroyed during the War, the area was left as a ghostly no-man's-land. A mass of corporate high-rise buildings, this metallic jungle still feels alien and isolated. However, Helmut Jahn's steel and glass Sony

Centre is an architectural draw and host to one of the city's largest entertainment complexes. Many of Berlin's major five-star hotels are also located close by. Just west of the development is the Kulturforum, home to the State Library and Berlin's Philharmonic Orchestra. In its distorted form, this sparkling gold edifice was based on the designs of Hans Scharoun.

Largely a residential area with little to lure in the tourists, Schöneberg is one of the more tranquil quarters of Berlin. Serving as a sedate buffer to Kreuzberg and a hip alternative to Wilmersdorf, it attracts a crowd of affluent intellectuals and chic thirty-somethings. Schöneberg translates as 'beautiful hill' – bizarre, considering it is completely flat. Much of the area's architecture dates back to the 19th century and an Altbauen style of building prevails – characterized by ornamental façades and balconies. It's a welcome antidote to the sterile concrete blocks of East Berlin. A farmers' market takes place every Wednesday and Saturday in the Winterfeldplatz. Cafés, bookshops and boutiques can also be found nestling among the surrounding streets. Since the 1920s, Schöneberg has been home to a lively gay community (mainly focused around Motzstraße), so it's not uncommon to see the symbolic rainbow flag displayed in many of the bar windows.

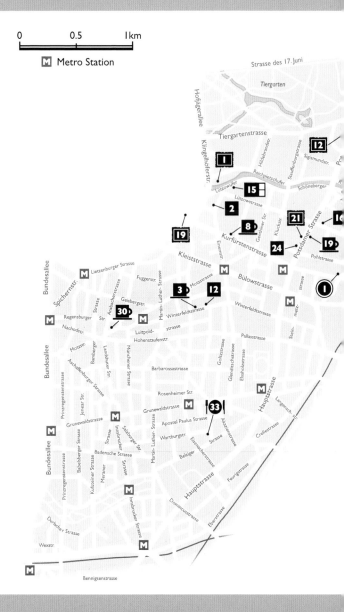

0   0.5   1km

Ⓜ Metro Station

CULTURE

1. Bauhaus
12. Philharmonie
19. Kleine Nachtrevue
21. Wintergarten Variete

DRINK

2. Bar am Lützowplatz
12. Green Door
16. Kumpelnest 3000
24. Victoria Bar

EAT

9. Facil
33. Storch

PARTY

1. 90°

SNACK

3. April
8. Café Einstein
19. Joseph Roth Diele
30. Tomasa

SLEEP

9. Grand Hyatt
15. Hotel Grand Esplanade
21. Madison
28. Ritz Carlton

sleep...

Hotel competition in Berlin is fierce. Investment by many four- and five-star hotels in the city has left smaller businesses struggling to match competitive rates and guests can generally enjoy good value for money – much better, in fact, than in any other major European city.

Berlin's main problem is a heavy West-side concentration of top-end hotels. The tourist industry has gradually drifted East since 1989, yet most hotel chains have failed to keep up. If you wish to stay in that area, try the intimate and romantic Honigmund or design-friendly Arcotel Velvet – both in Mitte. The SAS Radisson group has also opened a very respectable five-star in the area, with a unique attraction: it's only hotel in the world with its own 25-metre aquarium. The area around the Gendarmenmarkt also has several good hotels.

The main concentration of hotels in West Berlin can be found around Bleibtreustraße and on the streets between Ku'damm and Kantstraße. These tend to be a mixture of the historical, characterful, luxurious and fashionably stylish. Newer hotels can be found around the futuristic Potsdamer Platz development.

The city's oldest and most famous hotels base their operations on a very traditional interpretation of luxury. The Adlon and the Savoy are swathed in opulent grandeur. In a similar but more discreet style are the Regent and Brandenburger Hof. There's a healthy trend for design hotels in the city, easily the most striking being newcomer Q!-Hotel, while Ku'damm 101 is another design masterpiece. Still modern but less self-consciously styled are the Dorint, Madison and Intercontinental. The latter two also boast two of the city's best restaurants.

Another notable trend is that of the art hotel. These premises loosely function as art galleries, with the idea that original works of modern art add a degree of sophistication to your stay. The Künstlerheim Louise is definitely the most interesting, with individually designed rooms. For unrivalled odd hotel experience, check in to the Propeller City Island where themed rooms include a 'Chicken Curry' and 'Goth' room. Truly outrageous.

Greater character and intimacy can be enjoyed in several of the city's *pensions*. The hotel/*pensions* Funk, Dittburner and the Hotel Garni Askanischer Hof are dripping with atmosphere; they are generally smaller and the service more personal.

All hotels in this section have their own bathrooms, and prices quoted range from a single in low season to a suite in high season. Many also offer seasonal deals and rooms can often be booked online.

Our top ten hotels in Berlin are:
1. Q!-Hotel
2. Brandenburger Hof
3. Dorint am Gendarmenmarkt
4. Madison
5. Ku'damm 101
6. Intercontinental
7. Ackselhaus
8. The Regent
9. Hotel Bleibtreu
10. Schlosshotel

Our top five hotels for style are:
1. Q!-Hotel
2. Brandenburger Hof
3. Ku'damm 101
4. Madison
5. Dorint am Gendarmenmarkt

Our top five hotels for atmosphere are:
1. Brandenburger Hof
2. Madison
3. The Regent
4. Schlosshotel
5. Ackselhaus

Our top five hotels for location are:
1. Dorint am Gendarmenmarkt
2. The Regent
3. Ackselhaus
4. Q!-Hotel
5. Arcotel Velvet

Ackselhaus, Belforter Strasse 21, Mitte
Tel: 4433 7633 www.ackselhaus.de
Rates: €66–160

There are two house to this apartment hotel: the first more traditional and the second overtly modern. Over a century old, the first house has several themed rooms – ranging from a floral inspired bridal room to a more male dominated gentleman's drawing room. All are characteristic and come with the bonus of personal kitchen facilities. A newer house (with lift) was designed along a water theme. As such, particular attention has been paid to bathroom facilities and materials used. While rooms are styled loosely along a retro theme, splashes of colour come courtesy of the owner's fascination with Indonesia. Great efforts have also been taken to maintain original features in the building – some over a hundred years old. There are also plans to turn the downstairs Club del Mar breakfast room into a full blown seafood restaurant. A spacious outdoor garden can also be reached via a small walkway over a water filled courtyard. Few hotels this side of the city can offer rooms with of comfort and individuality – the Ackselhaus is an exception. Fantastic value.

Style 8, Atmosphere 8, Location 8

Adlon Hotel, Unter den Linden 77, Mitte
Tel: 22610 www.hotel-adlon.de
Rates: €280–8,500

Once the most luxurious hotel in the world, the Adlon opened
its grand doors in 1907 with support from Kaiser Wilhelm II. The
original building burnt down after World War II and the new
Adlon opened in 1997. Located next to the Brandenburg Gate
and Berlin's diplomatic quarter, it's a popular choice for heads of
state and deemed fit enough for the Queen – who opted for the
Adlon on a recent trip to Berlin. On the down-side, the entrance
is always swamped with tourists, although frosty door staff do
their best to deter non-residents. The rooms (337 in total) are
grand, but relatively characterless, and appeal to the more gen-
teel. Two bullet-proof presidential suites, however, would suit any
professional on Her Majesty's service and are truly palatial.
Upstairs, the exclusive Chinese restaurant is open to members
only – but worth a visit if you have the connections, as the food
is sensational. Downstairs, the upmarket Felix functions as a bar,
restaurant and club space.

Style 7, Atmosphere 7, Location 8

Albergo Die Zwölf Apostel, Hohenzollerndamm 33, Wilmersdorf
Tel: 868 890   www.12-apostel.de
Rates: €88–108

A love of all things Italian has inspired this romantic hotel. Its grand façade with ornate Renaissance trimming would be more at home in Verona than the drab streets of West Berlin. Inside, rooms are small but pleasant with plush red bedspreads and fairy-tale furnishings. Artworks are of Italian design and bring a touch of the Florentine to the household. Popular with a domestic German crowd, who seem fascinated with Europe's wayward boot, the hotel is quiet and guests are largely left to their own devices. Downstairs a popular restaurant serves, rather unsurprisingly, pizza. Deals run throughout the week and a sister branch can be found at Savignyplatz. The location isn't up to much unless you plan to explore the largely uneventful backstreets of West Berlin.

Style 7, Atmosphere 7, Location 6

Arcotel Velvet, Oranienburger Straße 52, Mitte
Tel: 278 7530 www.arcotel.at
Rates: €110–195

This new design-friendly hotel bears testimony to the changing face of Mitte – it was once the centre of Berlin's squat party phenomenon (Tacheles, the area's last remaining squat, can be found next door), but now gentrification has taken root (on the other side lies a branch of upmarket restaurant Lutter and Wegner). If you really want to be in the thick of the action, however, this is an ideal choice. Many of the rooms face onto the street below with floor-to-ceiling windows. When the sun shines, the building fills with light and guests benefit from the perfect vantage-point to watch life on the streets of young Berlin below. Draped muslin between bed and bathroom help create an airy space. The design is smart but simple, and the hotel attracts a young crowd. Although there is no restaurant, there are plenty of great places to eat in the area.

Style 8, Atmosphere 7, Location 8

Art'otel Ermelerhaus, Wallstrasse 70–73, Mitte
Tel: 240 620   www.artotel.de
Rates: €130–260

This peaceful residence is a hotel of two halves; rooms are filled with contemporary artworks from Georg Baselitz while an original breathtaking rococo ceiling can be found in the conference room. Overlooking the Spree, and halfway between Potsdamer Platz and Mitte, the hotel is something a of city-centre backwater. Rooms are tasteful and modern, and guests are invited to choose between colour schemes: red, green, blue or aubergine. Of the 109 rooms, 10 art suites have a balcony and two a kitchen. Staff are helpful and conduct business at an efficient but relaxed pace. The quirky hotel bar and restaurant is awash with Pop Art motifs, and although empty of an evening, it offers a refreshing start to the day. The older wing of the building is usually reserved for conference events, but it's worth sneaking a look.

Style 8, Atmosphere 7, Location 8

Artist Riverside Hotel, Friedrichstraße 106, Mitte
Tel: 284 900 www.great-hotel.com
Rates: €40–400

Meeting hotel owner Uwe Buttgereit explains a lot about this quirky riverside enterprise. The amount of gold in the lobby alone could dazzle in the dead of night. At best vaudeville, at worst Pat Butcher's jewellery box, this wonderfully tasteless building is too ridiculous to resist. Uwe attracts a crowd of actors and artists whom he hopes (and so do we) will usher in an air of creativity: a piano can be found downstairs in the

bar/café, and guests are invited to tickle the ivories. The rooms are actually extremely spacious, with fantastic views over the Spree; few other hotels offer such intimacy and comfort. Free-standing baths are especially romantic and can be filled with essential oils and rose petals at the guest's request. One suite boasts a particularly dramatic cinema projector. There are also plans to open a sauna, with views (again) to the river.

Style 6, Atmosphere 8, Location 8

Brandenburger Hof, Eislebener Strasse 14, Wilmersdorf
Tel: 214 050 www.brandenburger-hof.com
Rates: €165–450

This elegant and truly exceptional hotel is a tranquil idyll with a city-centre postal code. Combining classical elements with mod-ern design, the turn-of-the-century mansion has a timeless appeal. Many of the contemporary Bauhaus furnishings have actu-ally been exhibited in New York's MOMA. Natural oak finishes and simple colour schemes bring instant relaxation and rooms smell wonderfully fresh. The conservatory Wintergarten provides a serene start to the day, while gourmet meals can be enjoyed in the fine dining Quadriga restaurant. Old-school devotees will undoubtedly be drawn to the library and wine cellar – where a resident sommelier offers wine-tastings. The Thalia beauty suite is small, but masseuse Ellen Brueder is highly respected within

the industry. The hotel has a family feel, and guests can expect first-class and individual treatment. No other hotel in Berlin has combined trend and tradition quite so successfully. A highly recommended member of the Relais & Chateaux group.

Style 9, Atmosphere 9, Location 8

Dorint Am Gendarmenmarkt, Charlottenstraße 50–52, Mitte
Tel: 203 750 www.dorint.de/berlin-gendarmenmarkt
Rates: €197–510

Oddly enough, the greatest (but by no means only) attraction in this luxury modern hotel is a fantastic ballroom with an illuminated floor. Once a GDR building owned by the Church, it underwent a Studio 54 reinvention that blended modern design with historic features – the crystals in the dramatic light fittings

are all original GDR – and is now a favourite with exclusive fashion parties. The design innovations continue throughout the Dorint, all refreshingly subtle and understated. Clean cut and calming lines can be found throughout and corridors have been fitted with shifting mood lights. For those especially grey Berlin days, the sauna has several SAD lamps. The larger suites are comfortable enough to be apartments and several humorous touches (pull a bedside cord to play a sweet dreams lullaby) give the Dorint a very human appeal. The Aigner restaurant also comes highly recommended and serves a menu of Austrian and German cuisine.

Style 9, Atmosphere 8, Location 8

Grand Hyatt, Marlene-Dietrich-Platz 2, Tiergarten
Tel: 2553 1234   www.berlin.hyatt.de
Rates: €180–3,500

Although located in the industrial and faceless landscape of Potsdamer Platz, the Grand Hyatt is both stylish and sophisticated. A comfortable median between garish regal residences and sterile design showpieces, it suits a cosmopolitan crowd of mixed ages. Slick matt black surfaces are interspersed with the odd well-selected work of art. Rooms are smart and comfortable and will please most tastes; the marble bathrooms add a touch of luxury, and the heated floors are a bonus of modern technology. A spa and fitness centre can be found on the top floor, with breathtaking views of the city. Restaurant Vox offers gourmet cuisine in a *feng-shui*–styled setting and is a popular choice with visitors to the nearby Philharmonie classical concert hall (see Culture). The Hyatt also offers a 'hotel within a hotel' floor where exclusive guests benefit from their own concierge and lounge area.

Style 7, Atmosphere 7, Location 7

Hecker's Hotel, Grolmanstrasse 35, Charlottenburg
Tel: 88900 www.heckers-hotel.com
Rates: €150–350

Close to the boutiques and restaurants of Savignyplatz, this simple but smart hotel enjoys a pleasant location. Initially built in 1965, it was last renovated in 1994. Lagging considerably in the design stakes, rooms are basic – you could be in your aunt's spic-and-span guest room instead of a downtown hotel. Much better are the two suites, known as the Tuscan and Colonial. As their

names suggest, both are thematically designed and individually hand crafted. Instantly homely, they are perfect for longer stays and come with Bang & Olufsen DVD TVs. Corridors are wide, spacious and flooded with natural light. Guests respect each other's privacy and the place always feels pleasantly empty. Downstairs, the Cassambalis House restaurant is filled with artworks and curios – all collected by the Greek owner.

Style 7, Atmosphere 7, Location 8

The Honigmond, Invaladienstraße 122, Mitte
Tel: 281 0077 www.honigmond-berlin.de
Rates: €89–159

There are two Honigmond hotels in Berlin; this is the more upmarket one. It's tucked away in the quieter backstreets of

Mitte, and so enjoys a peaceful but central location. Wooden rafters and four-poster beds in several of the rooms give the Honigmond a romantic charm somewhat lacking in other Berlin establishments. Rooms are all unique; the more striking ones can be found in the hotel's oldest wing, dating back to 1845. Winding oak staircases lead up to each floor and decorative touches – such as suits of armour – create a stately atmosphere. Downstairs, a pleasant breakfast room looks out onto a Tuscan-style garden where several apartments are also available. Particularly pleasant is the largest of the garden apartments, which benefits from its own sun terrace and water fountain. Best of all, this regal residence, fit for a king, comes at a price his subjects can also afford.

Style 7, Atmosphere 8, Location 8

Hotel Art Nouveau, Leibnitzstrasse 59, Charlottenburg
Tel: 327 7440 www.hotelartnouveau.de
Rates: €95–230

Each of the rooms in this converted townhouse has been designed with artistic flair according to a different theme. In the 'Red Room' bed-heads have been fashioned in the form of ring-bound notepads, while the 'Yellow Room' is an uplifting mix of soft furnishings and strict angles. In the beige 'Literary Room' Bertolt Brecht's pontifications on enjoyment adorn a wall tapestry. The English-speaking owners have accumulated antique furnishings over the years. Rooms in the rear of the building are quieter, except when children fill the nearby playground. Guests are invited to keep track of their own drinks at an honour bar in the lobby and a well-stocked fridge is a tempting source of midnight snacks. Hardwood floors can be a little squeaky, but you'd do well to find such a charming hotel for this price. Intimate and unique.

Style 8, Atmosphere 8, Location 7

Hotel Bleibtreu, Bleibtreustraße 31, Charlottenburg
Tel: 884 740 www.bleibtreu.com
Rates: €137–262

Part of the Design Hotel chain, the Bleibtreu ultimately appeals to a younger crowd. All products used to build the hotel are biodegradable, with furnishings free from chemical treatment and wool carpets pollutant-free. Each floor has also been assigned its own smell – although, as with the Emperor's new clothes, it's hard to detect anything. The interior is tasteful and modern without being uncomfortably hip. Controversial works of art, such as Elvira Bach's sexually explicit wall tapestry, appeal to an unshockable and more *avant-garde* crowd. Mobile phones (communication range within the hotel only) are also provided for customer use, while breakfast in bed can be ordered via the TV remote. A New York deli, espresso bar and flower shop (with 31 different types of rose) can be found on site. A spa with personal trainer service, massage and colour light therapy is also open to guests.

Style 8, Atmosphere 8, Location 8

Hotel Garni Askanischer Hof, Kurfurstendamm 53, Charlottenburg
Tel: 881 8033
Rates: €95–200

There's an undeniable sense of tradition about this charming guesthouse. Admittedly the hotch-potch selection of furnishings doesn't hit high on the style scale, but idiosyncratic touches – such as stuffed toys lodged in the speaker of an antique grama-phone – are likely to raise a smile. Complete with embroidered

tablecloths and velvet-covered easy chairs, the breakfast room is stuck in a turn of the century time warp. Rooms boast an equally interesting selection of awkward antiques and fascinating curios. Many are remarkably spacious. Friendly service tops off the wonderfully esoteric experience.

Style 7, Atmosphere 8, Location 7

Hotel Grand Esplanade, Lützowufer 15, Tiergarten
Tel: 254 780 www.esplanade.de
Rates: €230–2,300

Flags from all over the world flutter in the grand courtyard of this business-friendly five-star hotel. In summer, tables are set out under the veranda within view of the Landwehr canal. Inside the hotel looks reputable enough, but lags somewhat behind newer design innovators in the city. Rooms can vary considerably, from the sober Le Corbusier studies to the oriental-inspired realms of relaxation. Several suites have open bathrooms with the bath in view of the bed to encourage social cleansing. Downstairs, the Harry's New York Bar is a tacky but popular night-spot. but conveniently it's within tripping-distance of bed. The Vivo restaurant serves up gourmet Italian cuisine. A small pool and sauna are also available for guests.

Style 8, Atmosphere 7, Location 7

Hotel-Pension Dittberner, Wielandstrasse 26, Charlottenburg

Tel: 884 6950 www.hotel-dittberner.de
Rates: €66–118

One of the best *pensions* in the city, the Dittburner is a lesson in classic West Berlin apartment living. Eclectic fine arts are taken from the gallery downstairs (also belonging to the hotel) and grand chandeliers dominate the hallways. Some of the rooms are palatial and the main suite – with raw silk *chaise longue*, Marianne Koplin bedside lamps and balcony – is truly magnificent. A wooden and glass lift transports guests to the third floor of this 1911 building, where rooms can be found. There's a sense of personal service in Dittburner, which is widely considered to be one of the most friendly hotels in Berlin, and you could be mistaken for thinking that you have walked into a private house. Elly Lange, owner since 1958, has taken great care with the upkeep, successfully meeting contemporary tastes in antique climes. Intimate and charming.

Style 8, Atmosphere 9, Location 7

Hotel-Pension Funk, Fasanenstrasse 69, Charlottenburg

Tel: 882 7193 www.hotel-pensionfunk.de
Rates: €34–113

This charming 1895 *pension* was once the home of Danish silent movie actress Asta Nielson. Although it was converted into a guesthouse in the 1950s, fortunately much of the building's original charm remains. Perhaps somewhat old-fashioned and shabby around the edges (the bathrooms require a little modernization), the place is still extremely graceful. The 14 comfortable rooms have been decorated with furnishings from the 1920s and '30s – collected over the years from auctions and antique stores. The carpets are quite dramatic and the abundance of pink can be overwhelming. Close to Gucci, Cartier and some serious shopping.

Style 7, Atmosphere 7, Location 8

Intercontinental, Budapester Straße 2, Charlottenburg
Tel: 26020 www.berlin.intercontinental.com
Rates: €195–2,100

At first glance, this mammoth hotel complex can appear impersonal and characterless. High-profile events often take place here, and a constant hustle of activity creates an upbeat buzz. But step inside the rooms and you'll quickly understand why the Intercontinental is such a popular choice; spacious and sleek, rooms offer mod-con comforts in pleasant surroundings. Larger suites are of a noticeably high quality and the enormous penthouse enough to impress even Britney Spears – just one of the Intercontinental's famous guests. The 'hotel within a hotel' floor offers guests an exclusive check-in and separate lounge for only a fractional amount extra (€50). The fantastic Michelin-starred Hugos restaurant can be found on the 13th floor, with views of Tiergarten and the Ku'damm: hotel guests are given priority table reservations (waiting can otherwise be up to a fortnight). The Intercontinental also offers one of the city's biggest 'wellness' centres, with warm water beds, ice showers and a large indoor pool. Large-scale luxury.

Style 9, Atmosphere 8, Location 7

Ku'damm 101, Kufürstendamm, Charlottenburg
Tel: 520 0550 www.kudamm101.com
Rates: €101–215

Subscribing to a minimalist ethos, it's hard to imagine this ultra-modern building was styled almost ten years ago. Husband and wife team Kessler + Kessler are responsible for the muted colourings which decorate each floor with elegant touches. Expect to find furnishings from young German designers, including tables from Munich's Lemongras Design Studio. Breakfast can be taken on the 7th floor, with fantastic views of the city. Alongside bread and butter, expect to find a remarkable selection of health foods. A well-equipped spa also offers massage, reflexology, shiatsu and ear acupuncture. In the evenings, DJs play in the lime green lounge bar. Ku'damm 101 is popular with a young and sophisticated crowd.

Style 9, Atmosphere 8, Location 8

Künstlerheim Louise, Luisenstraße 19, Mitte
Tel: 284 480 www.kuenstlerheim-luise.de
Rates: €82–149

Often referred to as 'a gallery where you spend the night', this
art-lover's paradise is less a place to lay your head and more a
sight to stimulate the mind and the senses. Each of the 50 rooms
has been decorated by a different international artist; they range
from the innovative to the utterly bizarre. The 'belle etage' lies in
the older part of the building – a neo-classical house dating back
to 1825. Rooms can be viewed and reserved in advance from the

hotel's website: Elvira Bach's *Three Women In Red* in Room 101 depicts a wall size image of (you've guessed it) three women against a red backdrop, while black-and-white pinstripes create a harsh optical illusion; stranger still is Christoph Platz's 'Standby' (Room 411) where 3D plaster casts of multicoloured socks have been glued to the wall; and Dieter Mammel's larger than life-size bed (Room 107) is yet to be rivalled. The hotel is situated close to East Berlin's biggest attractions.

Style 8, Atmosphere 7, Location 8

Madison, Potsdamer Straße 3, Tiergarten
Tel: 5900 50000   www.madison-berlin.de
Rates: €130–490

Popular with film crews and discerning trend-setters, the Madison presents a fresh and contemporary approach to hotel design. There's a certain youthful dynamism about the place that makes it instantly appealing; staff are young, interiors stylish and facilities generous. A small but serene spa can be found on the 11th floor, with great views over the city. The fantastic Facil restaurant, housed beneath a retractable glass roof, offers one of Berlin's finest dining experiences (but note: it is not open at weekends). Cocktail loungers, meanwhile, are well catered for with the Qui bar – which attracts guests from both within and outside the hotel. The philosophy at the Madison is to re-create the comfort of home in stylish surroundings you could probably never afford. Perfect if you plan to spend more time in your

hotel room than out. All the suites can be found on the top floor.

Style 9, Atmosphere 9, Location 7

Mövenpick Hotel, Schöneberger Straße 3, Kreuzberg
Tel: 230 060 www.moevenpick-hotels.com
Rates: €180–245

Owned by the Swiss Mövenpick group, this 243-room, four-star hotel is part of an old Siemens building erected in 1910. Close to Potsdamer Platz and the Sony Centre, the hotel is conveniently located halfway between East and West Berlin making it an ideal choice for those keen to explore both halves of the city.

It's also the only worthwhile hotel in the night-time mecca of Kreuzberg. Rooms are bright and airy with a retro design ethic – fire, water and air providing a loosely elemental theme. Admittedly furnishings are upmarket Ikea, but at least design hasn't come at the expense of practicality and comfort. The hotel restaurant can be found in an inner courtyard below a glass roof, and small sauna and fitness areas are also available. The real jewel in Mövenpick's crown is the fantastic Anhalter bar: a kaleidoscope of colours, whose space-age design falls somewhere between *Barbarella* and *Willy Wonka and the Chocolate Factory*. The bar stays open until 2am and attracts non-residents.

Style 8, Atmosphere 7, Location 7

Myers Hotel, Metzer Straße 26, Prenzlauer Berg
Tel: 440 140 www.myershotel.de
Rates: €80–165

Tucked away in a courtyard along a quiet street in Prenzlauer Berg, the Myers hotel offers simple but stylish hospitality in a warm and friendly environment. A gallery space and tranquil garden put this a cut above other hotels in the area. Both are ideal places to relax and couldn't be further removed from a stuffy hotel lobby. Although the hotel itself is only five years old, the building was once a traditional Berlin townhouse. The rooms are clean and pleasant, but – given the potential for this building – are disappointingly bland. But with the streets of Prenzlauer Berg on your doorstep, there's plenty of character close by.

Style 7, Atmosphere 7, Location 8

Propeller City Island Hotel, Paulsborner Strasse 10, Wilmersdorf
Tel: 891 9016 www.propeller-island.com
Rates: €65–189

If you tend to tire of hotel interiors easily, we challenge you to take on the Propeller City Island. Artist Lars Stroschen initially rented out four rooms as a means of earning some extra income, but demand was so high an entire hotel evolved. Each of the 45 rooms is unique – a figment of his sometimes warped and always unpredictable imagination. In the 'Flying Room' a bed is suspended over a floor at a 45° angle; in the 'Goth Room' a family of four can sleep in coffins; in the 'Upside Down Room' furniture is glued to the ceiling, with beds built into the floorboards; while the 'Dwarf Room' is just 1.40m high and home to several plastic gnomes. Each of the rooms also contains a six-channel radio featuring frog calls recorded by the artist in Bali. All rooms can be viewed on the website and guests can even swap for no extra cost for stays over four nights. Only in Berlin.

Style 9, Atmosphere 8, Location 6

Q!-Hotel, Knesebeckstraße 67, Charlottenburg
Tel: 810 0660 www.loock-hotels.com
Rates: €140–420

Berlin's premier design hotel, Q! opened in 2004 to a fanfare of favourable reviews. Whether you could actually stay here for a long period of time is questionable, but in terms of style this innovative hotel cannot be beaten. Walls meld into desks and ceilings while streamlined surfaces wrap around rooms to create a cocoon-like feeling. So fluid is the space that door handles and light switches are actually tricky to locate. Absolute white and smoked-oak wood form the colour schemes, with beds built into a block alongside baths. If at all possible, the communal areas are even more dramatic; red linoleum-clad surfaces glide through the bar, where ex-Met bar manager Ben Reed was drafted in to mastermind the cocktail menu. Downstairs, a spa benefits from hot sand floors and an atmosphere permanently set to body-temperature to boost the immune system. Q! is the handiwork of L.A.-based firm Graft, whose long list of clients includes Brad Pitt.

Style 10, Atmosphere 8, Location 8

Radisson SAS, Karl-Liebknecht-Straße 1, Mitte
Tel: 238 280 www.radissonsas.com
Rates: €160–650

Although it's part of a mammoth international chain, there's something unique about the five-star Radisson SAS Berlin – namely the world's largest cylindrical tropical aquarium, stocked with 2,500 exotic tropical fish. Rising 25 metres high, all interior-facing rooms boast an ocean view of the structure. Those preferring a taste of the real thing should ask for one of several rooms overlooking the River Spree and Museuminsel or just head straight to the swimming pool and sauna. Designed by Yasmine Mahmoudieh, each of the 427 rooms has a fresh and contemporary feel and a watery theme – six photographers were commissioned to take the water-inspired pictures used to decorate the rooms. Guests have a choice of two restaurants: either the oriental-style noodle bar or world-fusion restaurant Heat. Both are design wonders. The hotel is ideally located in the East close to many of the museums and opera houses. The only real down-side is the crowds; visitors to the neighbouring

Sealife Centre unfortunately have access to the hotel's
Aquarium.

Style 8, Atmosphere 7, Location 8

The Regent, Charlottenstraße 49, Mitte
Tel: 20338 www.regenthotels.com
Rates: €325–2,750

Also owned by the Radisson group, the Regent attracts a much
more exclusive client base. Staff are trained to be discreet, and
many celebrities and rich-list regulars enjoy the anonymity granted within these walls. When it comes to comfort and luxury, no
expense has been spared, and hotel staff will readily meet every
need without being overbearing. Once inside, the sense of calm
is instant and guests are invited to use the space as their own

for the duration of their stay. Although opulent, the classical design is tasteful, with extravagant chandeliers dominating the hallways; rooms are decorated in a colonial style. Surprisingly, the hotel only dates back to 1996. Chef Christian Lohse offers a fantastic gourmet menu in the hotel restaurant – one of the top seats in Berlin. Overlooking the Gendarmenmarkt, the Regent is close to Berlin's historical attractions. Unrivalled service.

Style 7, Atmosphere 7, Location 8

The Ritz Carlton, Potsdamer Platz 3, Tiergarten
Tel: 337 777   www.ritzcarlton.com
Rates: €250–5,000

A recent addition to the Potsdamer Platz multiplex of hotels, this sandstone skyscraper promotes luxury with a capital L. Unfortunately, opulence comes at the expense of taste, making the hotel popular with tourists whose idea of style translates as an all-in-one Louis Vuitton jumpsuit. Cascading marble stairwells in the German imperial style are perhaps a step too far, but sticklers for tradition will love the lavish display. Designer Peter Silling was inspired by renowned Prussian architect Karl Friedrich Schinkel. Attention to detail has been paid with every furnishing – with imported crystal light fittings (from Kalmar and Swarovski) and fine wood tables (from Boffi in Milan). But to the untrained eye, it's all simply very grand. The Debrosses bistro downstairs offers delicious fresh pastries; in a quest for authenticity all fittings

were actually taken piecemeal from an 1875 brasserie in France. Afternoon tea and cakes are also served in the lobby area.

Style 6/7, Atmosphere 7, Location 7

The Savoy Hotel, Fasanenstrasse 9–10, Charlottenburg
Tel: 311 030 www.hotel-savoy.com
Rates: €142–355

The first grand hotel in Berlin, the Savoy relies heavily on past glories. Having survived World War II almost intact, it was used as a domicile for the British headquarters in 1945–46. A hub of celebrity activity, the hotel's best suites are named after two favourite patrons: Henry Miller and Greta Garbo. These suites mirror each other in negative: one is black and the other white. Marble pillars are trimmed with gold and the rooms reflect a truly extravagant '40s style. Sadly, the hotel's standard rooms are far less impressive. The drab lavender colourings do little to bring the Savoy into the 21st century and give the impression of an ageing department store. However, cigar lovers will not be disappointed: the adjacent Times Bar is one of only 90 shops worldwide licensed to sell Cuban Havana Cigars. Guests can also store their new purchases inside a walk-in humidor. A faded beauty.

Style 6, Atmosphere 7, Location 7

Schlosshotel in Grunewald, Brahmstraße 10, Grunewald
Tel: 895 840   www.schlosshotelberlin.com
Rates: €275–3,000

Easily the most exclusive hotel in Berlin, this restored 14th-century villa can be found on the edge of the Grunewald. It's about a 15-minute drive from the Ku'damm, but the type of people staying here probably have their own limo at their beck and call. If not, the hotel staff will eagerly arrange one for you. The setting is stunning – particularly in summer when meals can be served on the lawn. A long driveway ensures ultimate privacy. King of *haute couture* Karl Lagerfeld was responsible for the opulent stately home interior. The decadent red lobby is particularly impressive and the restaurant highly recommended. A charming fairy-tale escape, although perhaps not overly practical for exploring the city.

Style 8, Atmosphere 8, Location 8

Westin Grand, Friedrichstrasse 158–164, Mitte
Tel: 20270   www.westin-grand.com
Rates: €131–1,950

Whether or not the classical style is your thing, you can't deny this five-star multiplex is the lap of luxury – if pastels and gold trims don't offend, the wonderfully comfortable surroundings will quickly please. At the very least, you know where your money's gone. Each of the 35 suites is themed with individual period décor, while the standard rooms are more traditional. Positioned on the corner of Friedrichstrasse and Unter den Linden, the hotel is ideally located close to East Berlin's designer shops and museums. The Westin Grand also offers a personal butler service – ready to deliver daily newspapers, shine shoes and even accompany guests on shopping trips. Guests can also relax in a pleasant garden patio, enjoying an evening drink in the sun. The Westin seems to follow the maxim that too much is never enough.

Style 7, Atmosphere 7, Location 8

Hg2 Berlin

eat...

Germany has never been head of the gastronomic table, but that's not to say Berlin's restaurants are below par. Although in the past the city has lacked a restaurant culture, in the last 20 years venues have sprung up across the city and there are now almost 2,000 to choose from. In the absence of any strong colonial links, Germans traditionally stuck to conservative domestic cuisine, but reunification helped ignite interest in international cooking; this has had a strong impact on both the type of food on offer and the variety of restaurant available, although Berlin still lags behind its European counterparts. Cheaper rents in the East have also allowed young entrepreneurs to set up their own creative ventures, which in turn attract a young and trendy crowd. Eating out is now rapidly becoming part of the Berlin social scene.

As a rule, restaurants in the West tend to be more established. Places such as Lubitsch and Florian in Savignyplatz have been around for quite some time and attract an upmarket crowd of actors and celebrities local to the area. That said, there's plenty of tradition to be found in the East. The food in Offenbach Stuben may not be to all tastes, but this intriguing dining room was a highpoint of elegance for the GDR. Russian restaurant Pasternak is also a haven of old East nostalgia.

The greatest explosion in restaurant openings has been around Mitte. These places are popular with a younger and more fashionable crowd, and the interiors fit accordingly. While style-conscious newcomers such as Zoe and Weinbar Rutz offer good food at a higher price, cheap eats such as Monsieur Vuong are equally popular with a similar crowd. If it's a lively and relaxed

atmosphere you're after, you could do worse than pizza parlour I Due Forni.

As with many capitals, the city's gourmet restaurants tend to be affiliated to hotels. While the majority are tailored towards an older generation, Hugos and Facil do well to keep the atmosphere fresh and vibrant. The team at E.T.A. Hoffman also endeavours to remove the stigma of stuffy affluence from gastronomy. Vau is one of the few independent gourmet restaurants.

Traditionally, Prussian cuisine has always been heavy on the meat (especially sausage) and vegetables. Good examples of German cooking can be found at Zander and Lutter und Wegner. Perhaps in envy of a Mediterranean climate, Berliners are obsessed with the Italian kitchen and over half the city's restaurants are Italian. Noi Quattro and Schwarzenraben are two of the best. Despite a considerable Turkish presence in Berlin, there are few formal Anatolian restaurants; the majority are stand-up snack stalls, Defne being the one exception. Easily the strangest dining experience in Berlin, is 'blind' restaurant Nocti Vagus – where guests are invited to eat in complete darkness.

As for tipping etiquette, a service charge of 17% is usually added automatically to the bill. It's not unusual for diners to split their bill and a waitress will always produce a calculator on request – even in the more exclusive restaurants. Never leave tips on the table, as this is considered quite rude, and if you hand a note over and say '*danke*' don't expect to receive any change back.

The prices given are for one person based on two courses with half a bottle of wine.

Our top ten restaurants in Berlin are:

1. Hugos
2. Vau
3. Svevo
4. Facil
5. Le Cochon Bourgeois
6. Storch
7. Paris-Moskau
8. Oki
9. Jules Verne
10. Engelbecken

Our top five restaurants for food are:

1. Hugos
2. Vau
3. Facil
4. Svevo
5. Borschardt

Our top five restaurants for service are:

1. Facil
2. Hugos
3. Vau
4. Offenbach Stuben
5. Nocti Vagus

Our top five restaurants for atmosphere are:

1. Le Cochon Bourgeois
2. Hugos
3. Storch
4. Pasternak
5. Engelbecken

Abendmahl, Muskauer Straße 9, Kreuzberg
Tel: 612 5170 www.abendmahl-berlin.de
Open: 6pm–1am daily   €44

There is quite literally an art to cooking at this colourful neighbourhood restaurant. Flamboyant owner Udo Einenkel has carved
himself a happy niche as a pastiche dessert-maker. Photographs of
his creations hang from the walls, each with their own title: a
honey ice-cream igloo decorated with the Soviet flag goes by the
name 'Cold War', while 'I Shot Andy Warhol' is a banana-shaped
mascarpone mousse dripping with a raspberry sauce. The list is
endless, and a mixture of locals and tourists come simply to mar-
vel at the bizarre collection. As for the actual menu, it's a mixture
of fish and vegetarian dishes. Most are mediocre and overpriced,
but nobody really seems to care; in Abendmahl it's all about leav-
ing room for dessert. In keeping with their kitsch reputation, the
restaurant also runs several themed nights – including an evening
where guests eat in complete darkness, and a murder-mystery
Hitchcock event. Tickets for both these must be purchased in
advance. An extraordinary experience – even if the food isn't.

Food 6, Service 8, Atmosphere 7

Borschardt, Französische Straße 47, Mitte
Tel: 2038 7110
Open: 11.30am-1am daily   €69

The history of this French bistro begins next door, where it originally opened as a delicatessen in 1830. In 1870 Borschardt's services were summoned as official caterer to the crown. Suffering extensive damage during the war, the restaurant lay empty during GDR times and was reopened in 1991. Borschardt retains much of its exclusive appeal and is now considered one of the top restaurants in Berlin. Attitudes are relaxed; guests can dress head-to-toe in denim and no one will bat an eyelid, except for the style aficionados. It's a popular choice for film crews and out-of-hours business acquaintances. Inside, the plush red banquettes are divided into several intimate booths, and, during the summer months, red sofas are even set up on the street.

Original marble columns and an intricately tiled floor hint at the opulence of bygone days. The mosaic of a Greek goddess behind the bar lay buried behind a brick wall for nine years – only eight of the stones are missing. Although the noise never dips below a din and service can be frustratingly rushed, the scene is energetic, which makes for an electric evening.

Food 8, Service 7, Atmosphere 8

Brot und Rosen, Am Friedrichshain 6, Prenzlauer Berg
Tel: 423 1916
Open: midday–open-end daily   €39

Ask any Berliner to recommend a restaurant and they'll probably suggest an Italian. Over half the city's kitchens serve from the

Med's back garden and the German obsession with pizza and pasta verges on the obsessive. Brot und Rosen is considered one of the better options and is often favoured by couples for a romantic dinner date. A little out on a limb, the restaurant overlooks the peaceful Friedrichshain Volkspark. On a sunny day, light spills through the large windows and a light lunch can last a peaceful eternity. Diners sit amidst pine dressers and yellow roses, beneath giant prints of Sophia Loren and other Italian goddesses and greats. The atmosphere is refined, but always laid-back and would suit almost every occasion. The food itself is slightly less impressive and consists mainly of standard Italian fare. Owner Peter Klann does, however, make his own organic oils, and at the back is a large gallery space where changing exhibitions are held.

Food 6, Service 7, Atmosphere 8

Chez Gino, Sorauer Straße 31, Kreuzberg
Tel: 6953 6961 www.sanremo-upflamoer.de
Open: midday–1am daily   €26

When you go down to the woods today, be sure of a big surprise… namely a sizable *Flammkuchen* (a traditional south German variation on pizza) or perhaps a bowl of home-made noodles. Bringing a taste of the Black Forest to Berlin (with a little French thrown in for good measure), Chez Gino offers a regional menu that is simple but tasteful. A sister enterprise to the successful Kreuzberg bar San Remo, the restaurant attracts a similarly young and vibrant crowd. Dishes may lack the finesse of a fine dining restaurant, but few spots are as cool to hang out in. Reflecting the rustic flavours of the kitchen, the interior follows a woodland theme; dark wood chairs look fresh from the carpenter's lathe and chunks of tree trunk have been fashioned into bookshelves. A final touch of the alfresco comes in the form of a forest mural filling the entire restaurant back wall. Elsewhere, original 1970s wallpaper from the local flea markets completes the kitsch touch. Great for large groups and not a teddy bears' picnic in sight!

Food 6, Service 8, Atmosphere 8

Le Cochon Bourgeois, Fichtestraße 24, Kreuzberg
Tel: 693 0101 www.le-cochon.de
Open: 6pm–open-end. Closed Sundays and Mondays.   €51

From the mass of creeping vines on the brickwork façade to the comical collection of pig ornaments inside, Le Cochon Bourgeious is one of the most charming restaurants in Berlin. It's a favourite choice for special occasions with all generations. The brightly painted dining rooms have a homely appeal and a meal at this upmarket French bistro is somewhat like a large-scale dinner party. A piano stands alongside the wood-carved bar and live music is played daily. Originally a row of shops, the restaurant opened seven years ago and chef Herr Berman has been serving middle-class Berliners ever since. Staff take pride in their work and offer a consistently good service. Great for romantics.

Food 8, Service 8, Atmosphere 9

Defne, Planufer 92c, Kreuzberg
Tel: 8179 7111
Open: 4pm–midnight daily   €29

For most Berliners, Turkish cooking extends no further than the doner kebab (which was actually invented in the city). Hoping to redress the balance and prove that there's more to Turkish cuisine than the ubiquitous elephant's foot, Defne serves classic Anatolian dishes using authentic ingredients from the local Turkish market. A far cry from the '*Imbiss*' kiosks so prevalent in

Kreuzberg, this sit-down restaurant offers more comfortable surroundings. The bare stone walls and tiled flooring lean toward more Mediterranean climes, while outdoor tables afford wonderful views of the river. On Fridays and Saturdays seasonal fresh fish is served, cooked by a traditional method over hot charcoal stones. Another speciality is *künefe*, a sweet cheese dish glazed with honey. Fresh and simply delicious.

Food 7/8, Service 7, Atmosphere 7

Engelbecken, Witzelbenstraße 31, Charlottenburg
Tel: 615 2810   www.engelbecken.de
Open: 4pm–1am Mon-Sat; midday–1am Sun   €37

A well-kept trade secret, Engelbecken is supposedly the establishment of choice for off-duty restaurant critics. Overlooking a peaceful lake, no other local restaurant boasts such serene surroundings. Specializing in Bavarian cooking, with several Italian-influenced dishes thrown in, the menu is mainly meat-based and the white sausages are a cholesterol-dripping favourite. Thankfully, several vegetarian and healthier options are also available, with a surprisingly good choice of salads. Sharing a similarly communal mentality to Storch, the simple wooden tables are often boisterous and always full. Even during the week queues have been known to snake outside the restaurant, so reservations are recommended. Amenable staff, however, will always do their best to accommodate, offering waiting guests a tipple from

the bar. Owing to the large volume of customers, service can be slow and slightly fraught, but once the food arrives, it's easy to forgive. Laid-back and lively, Engelbecken sits somewhere between restaurant and gastro pub. Visit once and it will quickly become your local.

Food 7, Service 7, Atmosphere 8

ETA Hoffman, Yorkstraße 83, Kreuzberg
Tel: 7809 8809 www.restaurant-e-t-a-hoffmann.de
Open: 5pm–open-end daily   €43

Chef Thomas Kurt and his kitchen are awarded maximum marks for effort. One of Germany's top chefs, Kurt hopes to rid fine dining of its exclusive image with his new restaurant venture in the ETA Hoffman hotel. Prices are reasonable without compromising on the quality of ingredients, and several set menu options are available. The restaurant also prides itself on its offering of a four-course vegetarian meal – practically unheard of in Berlin. So far, Kurt's efforts have been met with success and the restaurant is consistently busy. In winter, the bright yellow

walls and hanging artworks lift the spirits, while in summer months drinks can be taken on the outdoor terrace. Despite the bargain price tags, guests are elegant and it's popular with all ages. Extremely helpful staff round off an evening worth a million dollars, at a fraction of the price.

Food 8, Service 8, Atmosphere 8

Facil, Hotel Madison, Potsdamer Staße 3, Tiergarten
Tel: 590 051 234   www.facil-berlin.de
Open: midday–3pm, 7–11pm. Closed Sat, Sun.   €100

The retractable glass roof of the stylish hotel restaurant can be opened on a summer's day for the ultimate urban alfresco dining experience. But even when the weather is less gracious, Facil remains one of the city's top restaurants. 'Light' is a theme that pervades both the airy interior and the menu. Chef Michael Kempf has created a series of dishes that weighs heavy on the taste buds but not the stomach. Staff are extremely helpful and always unassuming; Facil aims to dispel any stiffness sometimes associated with gourmet restaurants. Instead, guests in jeans are welcomed as warmly as those in dressed up to the nines so, just like the Hotel Madison, Facil attracts a younger, stylish crowd. Unfortunately, as it's closed at weekends, most of the diners are hotel guests. Lavish but light-hearted dining.

Food 9, Service 9, Atmosphere 7

Florian, Grolmanstraße 52, Charlottenburg
Tel: 313 9184   www.restaurant-florian.de
Open: 6pm–3am daily   €50

Once a popular celebrity haunt, Florian remains a favourite with a luvvie theatre crowd and several West Berlin notaries. Perhaps relegated by some to last season's side of the wardrobe, Florian still attracts an interesting clientele who create an electric atmosphere. The room itself is simple yet elegant, with a '40s-styled cocktail bar; if Sam were here, Humphrey Bogart would most definitely ask him to 'play it again'. It's owned by two women from Franken, in the northern part of Bavaria, who base the menu on their local cuisine – heavy on roast meats and fish. Despite resting on its once-great reputation, Florian is still an old-school favourite. Turn up late to find a few showbiz regulars propping up the bar.

Food 8, Service 7, Atmosphere 7

Gugelhof, Knaackstraße 37, Prenzlauer Berg
Tel: 442 9229 www.gugelhof.de
Open: 4pm–1am Mon–Fri; 10am–1am Sat, Sun   €40

An impromptu visit by Bill Clinton put this neighbourhood restaurant on the map, but there are plenty of better reasons to dine at Gugelhof. Serving traditional Alsatian fare with a refined touch, the food is hearty without being heavy. Of particular note is the *Sandgauer Raclette*, a type of fondue prepared by diners at their own table. Brown and beige distressed walls create a warm and instantly relaxing interior and Gugelhof is remarkably laid back for a fine dining restaurant. The long rustic tables are ideal for large groups and peels of laughter keep the atmosphere upbeat. For young Berliners, this is the place to go when the parents are in town. Elevated above the leafy streets of Prenzlauer Berg, window diners benefit from a fantastic view. At weekends brunch is served and outdoor tables fill up quickly in good weather.

Food 7, Service 7, Atmosphere 7

HH Müller, Paul Linke Ufer 20, Kreuzberg
Tel: 6107 6760
Open: 8pm–midnight Sun–Fri; 6pm–1am Sat   €49

This industrial, canal-side building was once an electricity factory which was built by architect Hans Heinrich Müller in 1924. Left derelict for several years, it was finally renovated as a restaurant three years ago. The vast space reaches 8 metres high and a second level of seating overlooks the dining area below. The original cage doors, which hang from the walls, help retain the industrial feel and provide an impressive view to diners on the mezzanine floor. The interior is modern but a recurring flame motif can appear a little tacky. Regardless, HH Müller continues to attract a fashion-conscious crowd from the world of media, particularly in summer when the outdoor deck overlooking the water is always full. An international menu is mirrored by the kitchen, which

tends to play a little safe with its dishes.

Food 7, Service 7, Atmosphere 8

Hugos, Hotel Intercontinental, Budapester Straße 2, Tiergarten
Tel: 2602 1263 www.hugos-restaurant.de
Open: 6–10.30pm. Closed Sundays.   €100

High expectations have delivered high results at this even higher-rise gourmet restaurant. Found on the 14th floor of the imposing Intercontinental hotel, Hugo's really is a room with a view. On a clear night, it's possible to pinpoint the city's well-lit landmarks, and guests are often only able to tear their eyes from the full length windows once the first of their dinner delights has arrived. Michelin-starred chef Thomas Kammeier continues to

impress with his intricate cooking methods and meticulous presentation. Sparkling silver cutlery and white linen table cloths complete the setting for an evening of pure indulgence. Smart without being overtly trendy, Hugo's rides the crest of the culinary cutting-edge. The staff are genuinely helpful and boast an impressive knowledge of fine food and even finer wines. An adjoining bar is perfect for pre-dinner drinks. Book ahead – tables are often reserved two weeks in advance, with priority given to hotel guests.

Food 9, Service 9, Ambience 9

I Due Forni, Schönhauser Allee 12, Prenzlauer Berg
Tel: 4401 7333
Open: midday–midnight daily   €23

Easily the coolest pizza joint in town, there's never a dead (or dull) moment at I Due Forni. Run by a group of Italian punks (who also own a sister restaurant 'Il Cassolare' in Kreuzberg), it's a rock'n'roll venture without compromise. Since it refuses to advertise as a matter of policy, I Due Forni's reputation has spread by word of mouth. The space is vast and rammed with tables, but guests seem to revel in the chaos and no one really minds if their pizza takes 20 or 40 minutes to arrive. Busy staff exude a 'don't mess' attitude, but that's all part of the no-frills charm. Scrawled messages, often of a political nature, cover the wall space along with posters of well-known revolutionaries. The

choice of pizzas is vast and often eclectic – even horsemeat is offered as a topping. Although occasionally burnt around the edges, these are good pizzas by Berlin standards. An Italian restaurant that dares to be different, I Due Forni serves up anarchy in a deep pan.

Food 7, Service 6, Atmosphere 8

Jolesch, Muskauer Straße 1, Kreuzberg
Tel: 612 3581 www.jolesch.de
Open: 10am–1am daily   €35

When the charismatic owner opened this opulent local eatery in 1991, she hoped to bring some Austrian flair to Berlin. The name is taken from Friedrich Thorberg's novel *Aunt Jolesch*, which is where the fairy-tale appeal begins. Coffees and breakfasts are served in a small salon, shielded from the street by a thick red curtain; adjoining wooden doors lead into a large banquet room, popular with evening guests. Large gilt-framed works of art and an ornate chandelier complete the noble surroundings. Jolesch appeals to a diverse crowd: you'll find old men studying a crumpled newspaper over a cappuccino while young couples explore an extensive wine list (with over 150 bottles from Austria, Slovenia, Hungary and the Tyrol, a lengthy exercise). Service is always wonderful, with many customers attracted by the owner's eccentric charms. As you may have guessed, *Wiener schnitzel* is a prominent feature in the traditionally Austrian menu.

Jules Verne, Schlüterstraße 61, Charlottenburg
Tel: 3759 1106
Open: 9am–1am daily   €39

Restaurateurs Tanya and Hassan (originally from Cairo and Beirut) embarked upon this venture with the intention of creating a restaurant as cosmopolitan as their ancestry. The menu fuses flavours from all over the world; one dish, for example, blends tuna, chilli and *wasabi* with a black-ink spaghetti, and the 'Around the World in 80 Days' breakfast is also popular. With very little capital behind them, the pair spent six months refurbishing the restaurant. Much of the decoration was given or borrowed; the giant *papier-mâché* poppies, which dominate the back

room, are taken from a theatre backdrop. Building the restaurant as their perfect utopia, the hardworking team decided to name the place after their favourite author. A further twist of fate came when Tanya happened to find a Jules Verne toy in a Kinder egg. Crafted with love and run with pride, the appeal of this well– turned-out neighbourhood restaurant is difficult to resist.

Food 8, Service 8, Atmosphere 8

Kasbah, Gipsstraße 2, Mitte
Tel: 2759 4361   www.kasbah-berlin.de
Open: 4pm–midnight. Closed Sundays and Mondays.   €41

In terms of climate and culture, Berlin is a world apart from sun-baked North Africa, but step inside Kasbah and you could be in the heart of Morocco. Owner Driss Haggoud, himself born in Fez, was inspired to open the restaurant after paying a visit to Momo in London. Less exclusive than its Soho counterpart, Kasbah is still popular with a fashionable crowd keen for a taste of far-flung cultures. Every effort has been taken to re-create the Moroccan experience, with all the furnishings imported directly from the motherland. Colourful silk cushions are scattered about the restaurant, with wooden screens providing ample seclusion. The only light in an otherwise cavernous interior cascades from decorative glass lanterns. All the staff are from Morocco and will happily demonstrate traditional dinner etiquette – including washing the hands with rose water before a meal. For a truly authentic taste, order one of several dishes prepared in the tajine. Kasbah is romantic and intimate.

Food 7, Service 8, Atmosphere 8

Kuchi, Gippstraße 3, Mitte
Tel: 2838 6622   www.kuchi.de   €38
Open: midday–midnight Mon–Thurs; 12.30pm–12.30am Fri–Sun

Until newcomer Sasaya came along, Kuchi could pride itself as the best sushi restaurant in Berlin. The style of cuisine inevitably draws a cool cosmopolitan crowd, but it's the quality of ingredients that compels many to return. Offering an authentic menu, the dishes are even good by Japanese standards. If your idea of East Asian cooking extends no further than a California roll or a *bento* box, then think again; along with fish, *makis* are also rolled with *yakitori* chicken hearts. Seats at the bar can be cramped, but are ideal for the lone diner. Bigger parties are seated at one of several stone tables and a downstairs *tatami* room is also available for private hire. Pop into Greenwich next door for an after-dinner cocktail. Kuchi's sister branch can be found on Kantstraße in Charlottenburg while the neighbouring take-away outlet offers home delivery.

Food 8, Service 7, Atmosphere 8

Lubitsch, Bleibtreustraße 47, Charlottenburg
Tel: 882 3756
Open: 10am–open-end Mon–Sat; 6pm–1am Sun   €34

The owner of this smart Savignyplatz bistro was once part of the waiting staff. Having gathered enough funds, she purchased Lubitsch but still continues to wait hand and foot on her customers. Mirrored walls, white marble floors and gold trim give the restaurant a high-class appeal and aptly complement its silver service reputation. Design team Kaikiefer were responsible for the interior and originally used Lubitsch as a company show-piece. Table decoration is meticulous, with fresh cut flowers delicately placed upon crisp white tablecloths. Frequented by Berlin's it-girls, who waft through the restaurant on their way to or from nearby exclusive boutiques, lunchtimes are particularly busy, while several regulars also stop by for an early evening spritzer at the small bar. The menu is seasonal although incorporates a few international dishes.

Food 7, Service 8, Atmosphere 7

Lutter und Wegner, Charlottenstraße 56, Mitte
Tel: 202 9540 www.lutter-wegner-gendarmenmarkt.de
Open: 11am–3am daily   €36

This successful long-running restaurant enjoys a special place in Berlin's cultural history. Once the house of writer E.T.A. Hoffman, it was here that the German name for fizzy wine – 'sekt' – was first coined. In more recent times, the restaurant has found fame with its award winning *Sauerbraten* – a traditional dish of beef marinated in vinegar. Offering German cuisine with an Austrian accent, Lutter und Wegner is popular with both tourists from nearby hotels and sticklers for restaurant tradition. While fine diners should opt for the restaurant, a cheaper menu can be found in the bistro next door. A basement wine cellar is especially romantic by candlelight, and provides a great space to sample some of the 700 wines on offer; the most expensive bottle will set you back almost €2,500. Several other branches of Lutter und Wegner have opened up around the city, which slightly dilutes the restaurant's credentials. Definitely a safe bet.

Food 7, Service 7, Atmosphere 7

Monsieur Vuong, Alte Schönhauser Straße 46, Mitte
Tel: 3087 2643
Open: midday–midnight daily   €22

Essentially a fast-food Vietnamese restaurant with a menu limited to two or three dishes, Monsieur Vuong is worthy of mention simply because everyone eats here. Table reservations are never taken and it's not unusual for queues to spill out into the street. But the turnover is fast, making Monsieur Vuong a popular

choice for revellers seeking some sustenance before heading out on the town – and there are plenty of fashionable bars within easy walking-distance. The crowd is young and trendy and the atmosphere as vibrant as the bright red interior. Statues of Buddha, incense sticks and white orchids also make for a taste of Asia in downtown Berlin. Look out for the tropical fish tank embedded in one of the back walls. In a city where cheap Thai and Vietnamese restaurants lurk at every corner, Monsieur Vuong remains the original and the best.

Food 6/7, Service 6, Atmosphere 8

Nocti Vagus, Saarbrücker Straße 36–38, Prenzlauer Berg
Tel: 7474 9123   www.noctivagus.de
Open: 6pm–1am daily.   €55

Sick of the sight of your dinner partner? Nocti Vagus could be an option. One of two 'dark' restaurants in Berlin (oddly they're only metres apart), Nocti Vagus was inspired by a similar venture in Zurich. The concept is that all diners eat in complete darkness, thus heightening the senses and giving a momentary indication of what it's like to be blind. All waiting staff are blind (or have partially impaired sight) but, contrary to popular belief, the chefs are not. Diners ease into the experience with a drink in the (lit) upstairs bar while they decide between a choice of menus (or boldly opt for the 'surprise' option) and are then led into the restaurant by an assigned carer. Once inside, the balance

of dependency instantly switches and even a trip to the loo requires assistance. Although some diners have been known to panic, for most it's an interesting experience. Many return several times, often with family groups in tow. Special events also take place, including improvised theatre, erotic readings and even a 'crazy night' where, according to organizers, anything can happen. Part social experiment and part fun, a visit to Nocti Vagus is certainly memorable, and the food's not bad either. Weird? Yes. Wonderful? Definitely.

Food 7, Service 9, Atmosphere 8

Noi Quattro, Strausberger Platz 2, Friedrichshain
Tel: 2404 5622 www.noiquattro.de
Open: midday–midnight Mon–Sat; 10am–midnight Sun   €38

Opening an upmarket restaurant in this traditionally residential area of town could be considered commercial suicide, but taking risks is what Noi Quattro does best. While other Italian restaurants stick to traditional dishes, chef Andreas Staack prefers to experiment with more radical Mediterranean flavours. A relative newcomer, Noi Quattro is slowly gathering a discerning following among native Italians and happy converts. Lunch deals are particularly good value and attract a business crowd prepared to travel the distance. The interior is clean, modern and elegant, which instantly calms the nerves. Although situated next to the vast Strausberger Platz roundabout, the restaurant is sufficiently

far enough from the road to keep traffic noise to a minimum. Staff are charismatic and vivacious, which makes for a thoroughly pleasant meal. Reliably smart and warmly welcoming.

Food 8, Service 8, Atmosphere 8

Oderquelle, Oderberger Straße 27, Prenzlauer Berg
Tel: 4400 8080 www.oderquelle.de
Open: 5pm–2am daily   €24

Largely overlooked by tourists, this friendly German *kneipe* (pub) is a well-kept local secret. Home-cooked German pub fare is served in laid-back and occasionally boisterous surroundings.

Food is of a reliable quality and the menu representative of traditional local cooking. Those opting for a full sit-down meal can be seated in either one of the large back rooms, while snacks can be taken at the bar. But don't arrive hungry; the wait for food can be long, bearing testimony to Oderquelle's claim that all dishes are made from scratch. Once an art gallery, this German take on the gastro pub has existed in its current state for the past 10 years. While other ventures along this street come and go, Oderquelle remains a safe bet. Lovingly weathered, the long wooden pews have seated bums of all shapes and sizes, from burly tattooed truckers to dapper media bods tired of self-conscious *szene* spots. Ideal for diners who prefer a pint of beer to a glass of wine.

Offenbach Stuben, Stubbenkammerstraße 8, Prenzlauer Berg
Tel: 442 7654 www.offenbachstuben.de
Daily: 6pm–open-end daily   €43

Once the finest place to dine in former East Berlin, Offenbach
Stuben proudly functions in a bizarre time warp. Wall or no Wall,
it's business as usual and this singular jewel in the GDR culinary
crown remains staunchly resistant to change. At a time when
peasant food prevailed in most households, Offenbach Stuben
would boast fine wines and prime cuts of meat. Thirty-five years
later, in today's climate, the same dishes can weigh on the
untrained stomach like a ton of lead. But nostalgic Ossies return
to savour a taste of yesteryear. The restaurant itself consists of
several small salons, each separated by heavy wooden divides.
(The building was once a pub and the back room the propri-
etor's bedroom.) Out of sight and barely within earshot, couples
whisper conspiratorially over flickering candlelight. The oddly
cobbled together interior consists mainly of antique theatre
props, all gifts from loyal patrons. Particularly famous is the music
box at the restaurant entrance, which was smuggled from West
to East Berlin – a dramatic gesture in itself. Friendly staff will
happily offer a demonstration on request. By no means the best
food in Berlin, but a real taste of history.

Food 5, Service 9, Atmosphere 7

Oki, Oderberger Straße 23, Prenzlauer Berg
Tel: 4985 3130
Open: 3–11pm. Closed Mondays.   €37

In Berlin, anything goes, so a restaurant fusing the traditional North German kitchen with Japanese cuisine should come as no surprise. Potato soup is served with *shitake* mushrooms and Edelfish soup with black sesame seeds. The concept may be strange, but it's certainly successful; Chef Otto Pfeiffer has even won awards for his innovative recipes. While travelling in Japan, he studied delicate traditional cooking methods and applied them to his own heavy home-grown ingredients. Each Sunday a special Japanese patisserie is also served. The restaurant itself is

small, but stylish and nicely formed. Plastic neon lanterns decorate the walls and the working kitchen is on display. Service is friendly and Otto is more than happy to wax lyrical about his unique culinary techniques. In the absence of any pomp and circumstance, the atmosphere is down-to-earth. Turn up in a pair of jogging bottoms and no one will bat an eyelid. Perhaps not the place for a flash dinner date, but refreshingly different in many respects.

Food 8, Service 9, Atmosphere 7

Parc Fermé, Wiebestraße 36–37, Tiergarten
Tel: 2061 3050
Open: 6–11pm. Closed Sundays and Mondays.   €70

Eating in a car parking lot may not exactly sound appealing, but
when that lot happens to be the exclusive Meilenwerk it's a very
different story. Four-wheel fanatics store their vehicles (from vintage cars to Lamborghinis) in this huge factory-like building. Parc
Fermé can be found towards the far end of the block and has a
separate external entrance. There are only five tables available
(each one decorated with a model car), so booking is essential.
The menu is classic fine dining, with an extraordinary list of
wines. Unlike the industrial building, Parc Fermé is a warm and
inviting space, but even a vast array of pot plants fails to detract
from the sometimes overpowering stench of diesel that occasionally seeps in. Still, for some it's heavenly and car enthusiasts
will be only too eager to skip dessert for a tour of the building.
Out on an extreme limb, Parc Fermé must be reached by car –
which shouldn't really be a problem.

Food 8, Service 7, Atmosphere 7

Paris-Moskau, Alt-Moabit 141, Tiergarten
Tel: 394 2081 www.paris-moskau.de
Open: 6pm–1am daily   €60

Once adrift in a gastronomic no-man's-land, this top-class restaurant has been brought closer into town by rapid urban development, but it is still relatively isolated and best reached by car. Lying beneath the railway lines, the timber building dates back to 1898. The interior is tasteful and art-deco inspired, and table space is limited, making the place feel both intimate and exclusive. Despite being a stickler for tradition, Paris-Moskau has a more modern feel than rival restaurants of similar age and calibre – partly thanks to the young and vibrant waiting staff. The kitchen specializes in regional German cooking with an emphasis on the finest ingredients. As you'd expect of a gourmet restaurant in Berlin, the clientele is slightly older. That said, Paris-Moskau is well received among foodies of all ages. A Berlin classic.

Food 8, Service 8, Atmosphere 8

Pasternak, Knaackstraße 22, Prenzlauer Berg
Tel: 441 3399 www.restaurant-pasternak.de
Open: midday–1am daily.   €43

When Pasternak opened its doors to the public in 1991, it was one of the first restaurants to start trading in this area. Formerly a 'Pasamt' (Passport Control building), it was a familiar meeting-point for the local Russian Jewish community. Owner Ilja Kaplan, himself a Russian Jew, chose to name the restaurant after Boris Pasternak, author of *Dr Zhivago.* Filled with antique lampshades, sepia-toned photographs and even a piano, the interior has been modelled to resemble the writer's 1930s living room. At night, candlelight makes for an intimate atmosphere and there are few restaurants to rival Pasternak in the romance stakes. Along with the warming smell of *szarkœ* (Russian stew, made Jewish-style) and traditional borscht, a sense of nostalgia hangs heavily in the air. Essentially comfort food, traditional dishes are netherthless prepared with delicacy and the menu (contained within a vintage photo album) lists some interesting combinations. The Sunday brunch is worth reserving a table for, when a buffet of traditional Russian fare is served. For more intimate occasions, ask for a table in the back room, hidden behind a thick red curtain.

Food 7, Service 7, Atmosphere 9

Sasaya, Lychener Straße 50, Prenzlauer Berg
Tel: 4471 7721
Open: midday–3pm and 6–10pm. Closed Wednesdays.   €29

If Sasaya is Berlin's current flavour of the moment, then *sake* and soy sauce are on everyone's taste buds. The eastside's hip squad has already granted their hallowed seal of approval and now every Tom, Dick and Helga is tripping over themselves to bag a table. A mix of lime green and orange, the interior is refreshingly modern, which suits the stylish clientele perfectly. Diners can choose to sit at a table, at the bar, or cross-legged on the floor; the latter option is extremely conducive to late night lounging and, despite the demand for tables, customers are never rushed. Thankfully, however, style is not at the expense of substance. Along with traditional Japanese cuisine, a range of regional specialities are offered. As with most Japanese restaurants, the success of your meal is in the selection; venture beyond the bento-

box standards and you'll be off to a good start. Unfortunately, much is lost in translation, so it's worth trusting the waiter's recommendations. The restaurant stands alone at the quieter end of Lychener Straße.

Food 7, Service 8, Atmosphere 9

Schwarzenraben, Neue Schönhauser Straße 13, Mitte
Tel: 2839 1698 www.schwarzenraben.de
Open: 11.30am–open-end Mon–Fri; 2pm–open-end Sun   €45

As it was a poor-house in the 18th century, the irony of Schwarzenraben's conversion to upmarket restaurant caused minor controversy among the politically correct when it opened. During the 1920s the premises were used as a cinema where men and women were seated separately; now a similar principle applies, but segregation is financial: cheaper meals and coffees are served in the café out front, while linen-draped tables at the back are reserved for fine diners. Classic Italian dishes are served, with an emphasis on game and fish, complemented by a good wine menu. Diners can disappear from view in the dark wood-panelled interior and the subtle low lighting makes for an intimate atmosphere. Staff can be po-faced, but are unobtrusive and every effort is undertaken to make each meal a special occasion. When weather permits, tables are also set in the restaurant's garden where a sculpture of Schwarzenraben's namesake black raven can be found. Perhaps a little past its prime, it's still one of the better places to eat out in Mitte.

Food 8, Service 7, Atmosphere 8

Spindler & Klatt, Kopenicker Straße 16–17, Kreuzberg
Tel: 6956 6775
Open: 8pm–1am Weds–Sun.   €35

While most young Berliners like to party, they're rarely prepared to fork out on a smart sit-down meal. That's something the Spindler Klatt team hope to change. Combining a stylish restaurant with a musically discerning dance-floor, this waterside warehouse has great ambitions. Formerly a storage house for grain and a printing works, the venue has been reworked from scratch. A cast iron construction unit still provides a casing for the customer toilets. The restaurant space is large and airy, with an ethnic inspired interior. Delicate muslin drapes divide the space and vast cushioned beds are a comfortable dining alternative to the standard table and four chairs. While admittedly limited, the menu is of a consistently good quality and service of a high standard. During the summer, tables are set outside along the riverfront. Inconspicuous at street level, the front door can be hard to find, but – like most hot spots in Berlin – that's exactly how the owners intend it to be.

Food 8, Service 8, Atmosphere 8

Storch, Wartburgstraße 54, Schöneberg
Tel: 784 2059 www.storch-berlin.de
Open: 6pm–1am daily   €46

The owners of Storch really have got it sussed; no restaurant can survive on food alone, but combine quality cooking with a convivial atmosphere and you're onto a winner. When Volker Hauptvogel opened Storch, he hoped to bridge the post-war gap between generations by bringing them together at one large wooden table. For the most part, his aims have been achieved. The restaurant doors are always open and diners from all walks of life are invited to rub shoulders. Once a member of a successful '80s punk band, Hauptvogel is well travelled and well known in the local community. His ethics are both commendable and sadly rare in Berlin, making Storch a unique enterprise. The rustic but sophisticated interior is instantly comforting and conducive to lively conversation. German, French and Alsatian food is served from a kitchen as smart as the restaurant itself (at Hauptvogel's insistence). Translated his name means 'chief of birds', and with management this egalitarian, it's easy to see why Storch has taken off.

Food 8/9, Service 7, Atmosphere 8

Svevo, Lausitzer Straße 25, Kreuzberg
Tel: 6107 3216   www.restaurant-svevo.de
Open: 6pm–open-end. Closed Sundays.   €49

Although Svevo is somewhat lost in the backstreets of
Kreuzberg, it would be criminal if this wonderful restaurant were
to be forgotten, since it's one of the few places in Berlin that
truly combines gastronomy with comfort. Owners Sven Reschke
and Silke Brandenburg learnt their crafts in powerhouse restaurants Hugos and Aigner. Frustrated by a lack of creative freedom,
they set out alone to offer guests high-class cooking at more
affordable prices. Using simple but fresh ingredients their menu
combinations could rival some of the finest dining spots in

Berlin. But, unlike more faceless establishments, the service in Svevo is both personal and intimate. A menu is wrapped as a scroll, while a list of wines can be found in a filing box. A sumptuous selection of breads arrives on a tiered cake tray – and that's before the meal has even started! Set menus are offered and true gourmets can also order an 'in-between' course. The cosy, but modern space attracts young couples and gentle conversation provides the only accompaniment to efficient kitchen clatter. Fine dining without the hassle.

Food 9, Service 8, Atmosphere 9

Vau, Jägerstraße 54–55, Mitte
Tel: 202 9730 www.vau-berlin.de
Open: midday–2.30pm, 7–10.30pm. Closed Sundays.   €100

One of Berlin's few gourmet restaurants independent of a five-star hotel, Vau has reaped deserved rewards since opening in 1997, and the restaurant continues to carry its one Michelin star. Founded on a philosophy of 'enjoyment for all senses' the owners really do make a meal of every dinner date occasion. The international menu has a strong focus on seasonal ingredients and provides ample opportunity for chef Kolja Kleeberg to demonstrate his culinary dexterity and flair. Over 480 wines are offered and a selection of digestives and cigars can be enjoyed in a pleasant basement wine cellar. The restaurant is modern and elegant and will appeal to most tastes. Service is friendly and

efficient, although delivered with a hint of teutonic precision. Guests should arrive smart and expect a gastronomic work-out like no other. Those on a budget should try Vau for lunch, where each course costs a mere €12.

Food 9, Service 8, Atmosphere 8

Weinbar Rutz, Chausseestraße 8, Mitte
Tel: 2462 8760 www.rutz-weinbar.de
Open: 5pm–open-end. Closed Sundays.   €65

It's hard to believe the outer walls of this bustling wine bar/restaurant are actually made of glass – floor-to-ceiling shelves are filled with bottles of wine from around the globe. Striking reds cast a syrupy hue across the downstairs bar, dotted with crisply laid tables and more casual bar stools. But the real action takes place on the second floor in the well-designed nouvelle cuisine restaurant. Chef Marco Müller experiments with a 'global aroma cuisine', creating fresh dishes with clever use of spices and herbs. The clean-cut and stylish space tends to attract an equally trendy and affluent Mitte crowd. Rutz is also considered a hot spot for an early evening glass of wine and light snack and business workers arrive in droves to loosen their ties and relax. Full bodied and full of life – the best wine address in Berlin.

Food 8, Service 7, Atmosphere 8

Zander, Kollwitzstraßee 50, Prenzlauer Berg
Tel: 4405 7678 www.gourmetguide.com/zander
Open: 6pm–open-end Tues–Sat.   €43

Specializing in regional dishes from Brandenburg, this family-run
business has earned itself a healthy reputation. Ingredients are of
a high quality, with Zander fish freshly caught from the Havel
river. Set and seasonal menus are offered, with lengthy explana-

tions of each dish. Every effort has been taken to educate diners
on the Brandenburg kitchen and helpful staff will happily advise
on combinations. The accompanying wine list is equally comprehensive. Dishes are prepared with precision, but are not neces-
sarily for the faint-hearted – offal and blood sausage feature
heavily. However, there are plenty of lighter fish options available.
The kitchen is open-plan and watching the cooks at work can be
fascinating. The restaurant is often booked for big parties,
although a mezzanine level provides ample space. The rather
conservative feel is lifted by the bright yellow interior, which
verges on the outrageous. Zander has won several national
awards and in an area awash with restaurants, it remains unrivalled in the gastronomic stakes. An interesting adventure in
German cooking.

Food 8, Service 8, Atmosphere 7

Zoe, Rochstraße 1, Mitte
Tel: 2404 5635 www.zoe-berlin.de
Open: midday–2am Mon-Sat, 5–11pm Sun.   €30

A fusion of international flavours awaits at this stylish new
restaurant opening; chicken breast is served with a chilli-lemon-
grass relish while Zander ravioli sits comfortably alongside a vegetarian curry. The two cooks hail respectively from Germany and
Malaysia. Dishes are ambitious, but executed well and guaranteed
to stimulate the senses. A series of white-linen-draped benches
lines the lime green walls and a curved bar forms the central
focus of an otherwise empty space. Design has been kept to a
style savvy minimum, which can appear slightly sterile in daylight.
On the plus side, guests never feel on top of each other – even
when the restaurant is full to capacity. Although still finding its
feet, Zoe is already attracting wanted attention from Berlin's tailored trendies. *Szene* restaurants in Berlin are rarely of this quality, making Zoe one to watch.

Food 8, Service 7, Atmosphere 7

Zur Henne, Leuschnerdamm 25, Kreuzberg
Tel: 614 7730
Open: 7pm–open-end. Closed Mondays.   €22

Frustrated with over-complicated foreign menus and the rigmarole of whipping out a phrase book every time you sit down to eat? Well, there's no risk of delaying a meal with fraught indecision at Zur Henne, because there's only one thing on the card and that's chicken! Half an organically reared, milk-roasted chicken to be exact. And unless you have an aversion to poultry (or eating with your fingers) you won't be disappointed. The succulent meat wrapped in a crisp coating would certainly wipe the Kentucky smile from Colonel Sander's face! The only decision you really need to make is whether to opt for potato salad or coleslaw (we'd go for coleslaw every time). The pub itself has been around for a ripe ol' 97 years and the heavy gold bar pumps have pulled plenty a pint. The timber framework and distressed walls create a warm nostalgic ambience and are almost as big an attraction as the spit roasts themselves. Neither grotty nor touristy, Zur Henne is still a fine example of a traditional German pub.

Food 7, Service 7, Atmosphere 7

drink...

The number of bars in Berlin is phenomenal and there's a huge variety to choose from – mainly because the scene remains refreshingly independent. In the absence of any big-name chains, each venue has its own distinct identity and character making this the perfect city for bar-hopping. Thanks to lax licensing laws, most bars operate an open-end policy, meaning they close when the last guest chooses to leave. During winter, places tend to close earlier but both White Trash and Kumpelnest 3000 are reliable late-nighters.

Berlin's main concentration of bars is in Mitte, Prenzlauer Berg and Kreuzberg. There's also a strong bar scene in Friedrichshain, although the majority of venues tend to attract students and backpackers. Travel further west to find the best cocktail bars. Places rapidly open and close so it's often hard to keep track of what's in and what's out of vogue. Several only open through the summer months. Recent years have seen the advent of 'city beaches', often with an accompanying bar. The Badeschiff is the most extreme and consists of a heated swimming pool suspended in the River Spree. Other summer-only spots worth checking out are Strandbar Mitte on Montbijoustraße and Schönwetter at Mauerpark in Prenzlauer Berg.

East Berliners tend to recall their squat party days with a certain amount of nostalgia and many bar owners have attempted to re-create those halcyon times. Bar Wohnzimmer is probably the best example, designed along the lines of an actual house; each room is decorated with a mish-mash of period furnishings. In fact, you'll quickly notice the majority of Berlin bars have a similar selection of shabby sofas and coffee tables. In part, this is an attempt to replicate a living-room environment; but it's also a cheap means of decking the place out, and most pieces are picked up at flea markets.

While some bars are simply good places to hang out, others are a phenomenon unto themselves. The Weinerei enterprises have proven extremely popular with an egalitarian crowd. Only wine is served and guests are invited to help themselves, paying only what they think to be appropriate. Taken with a heavy dose of irony, White Trash has also developed something of a cult following.

There are several excellent cocktail bars in Berlin, guaranteed to suit all tastes, with the more sophisticated joints found in the West. The Victoria bar is currently considered to be the best, while Green Door follows shortly behind. Both Fluido and Greenwich attract a younger and more casual crowd.

In terms of design, several venues are worth a visit for their interiors alone. The KMA, a glass-box structure on the Karl-Marx-Allee, is a striking example of GDR architecture. Part of a Bauhaus structure, the Schaubühne, the Universum Lounge was given its space-age renovation by German design firm Player and Franz.

The traditional German pub is referred to as an *Eck kneipe*, and the majority are found on street corners ('*Eck*' translates as 'corner'). For the most part, they are fairly unremarkable and full of old men. Other examples of old-worldly charm can be found at Bellman and Würgeengel.

103, Kastanienallee 49, Prenzlauer Berg
Tel: 4849 2651
Open: 9am–open-end daily

A bold statement on the Kastanienallee, this trend-sensitive bar
is the most extreme (and popular) on the stretch. At weekends,
Berliners flock here to indulge in an otherwise unspectacular
brunch. Still, with looks this good, a few burnt pieces of toast can
easily be forgiven. The retro-inspired bar fittings and citrus-
coloured seating are pure design magazine material; oversized
flower vases litter the room, vying for aesthetic attention with
the wispy catwalk models serving behind the bar. Don't expect
service with a smile – in 103 it's always sultry. At night the pace
picks up with a prowling fashion circus of intensely styled
jeunesse dorée.

Bar am Lützowplatz, Lützowplatz 7, Tiergarten
Tel: 262 6807   www.baramluetzowplatz.com
Open: 2pm–4am daily

Sixty minutes can last an eternity at this classic cocktail bar –
especially if you turn up between 2 and 9pm when Bar am
Lützowplatz hosts the longest happy hour in the world. It claims
to serve the best Mai Tai to be found anywhere (apparently it's
all about getting the measures right) and, as further enticement,
the bar is a champagne-devotee's paradise, with 126 to choose
from. A perennial favourite with pretty much everyone,

Lützowplatz does exactly what it says on the packet – the cocktail selection is all about the classics and more freestyle innovations are kept to a minimum. The long cocktail bar stretches into infinity, with a collection of Le Corbusier easy chairs at one end

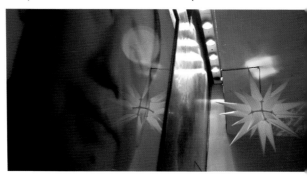

of the room. Made entirely of wood and steel, it's hard to believe the timeless interior was conceived almost 14 years ago.

Le Bar Du Paris Bar, Kantstraße 152, Charlottenburg
Tel: 3101 5094 www.parisbar.de
Open: 7pm–3am. Closed Mondays.

A see-and-be-seen classic, where the glamour of its starry regulars is one of its greatest allures. Although a bistro with a French kitchen, many guests come here simply to drink in the buzz – and, of course, a cocktail or two. Unlike the legendary Paris Bar

restaurant next door, it's possible to get a table without booking weeks in advance. Owner Michel Wurthle opened this sister venture as an overspill to the favourite celebrity haunt, and a similar melée of actors, artists and musicians pass through its doors, which are equally open to those who don't grace the TV screens – while the clientele might be exclusive, the door policy is not. Arrive late to rub shoulders with some of Berlin's finest – any earlier than 1am and you may be disappointed. If possible, book ahead for a table at the restaurant next door where the crowd and atmosphere are even more electric.

Bar Nou, Bergmannstraße 104, Kreuzberg
Tel: 7407 3050 www.bar-nou.com
Open: 8pm–3am daily

Although a hub of activity by day, the pretty Bergmannstraße is strangely quiet by night save for this hip and colourful cocktail bar. Located in the cellar, the space is awash with warm red and syrupy orange lights designed by a local artist. Seating is either at the bar or on one of the beige leather sofas in the rectangular

lounge room. Of the 150 different cocktails on the menu the most popular choice is the Papa Hemingway, a concoction of white rum, lime, grapefruit, cane sugar and maraschino. Music – mostly Latin, lounge and jazz – comes courtesy of a well-stocked mp3 system. The bar is popular with all ages and anyone who's up for a party. Measures are generous – particularly as the night wears on.

Bellman, Reichenberger Straße 103, Kreuzberg
Tel: 6128 0334
Open: 6pm–open-end daily

Distressed walls illuminated by candlelight and an imposing wooden bar make Bellman a favourite for film location scouts. A working-class bar since the 1920s, Bellman is popular with an old-school Kreuzberg crowd. Dinner – a mixture of Italian and

Russian cooking – is served at the weathered wooden tables, but later in the night it's standing room only as the place quickly fills up. A shelf behind the bar is filled with tattered records and the evening's playlist is at the whim of who's serving at the bar but, for the most part, nothing beyond 1979 gets a look in. Bellman shares strong connections with bar Würgeengel – in terms of both staff and nostalgic atmosphere.

Club der Visionäre, Am Flutgraben 1, Treptow
Tel: 6951 8944 www.clubdervisionaere.com
Open: 4pm (midday Sat/Sun)–open-end daily

Along with nearby Badeschiff and Freischwimmer, this riverside bar and trendy hang-out is a popular summer location. Closed during winter months, it only opens once temperatures start to rise – usually in spring. Essentially a wicker shack, it always attracts a cool crowd who hanker after an understated ambi-

ence. Preferring to shun public exposure in favour of an underground status, you're unlikely to find Club des Visionäre mentioned in the local listings. Everyone in the city, however, knows the bar exists and the place is actually far more commercial than the owners might like to imagine. Cushions are scattered about the deck, while a traditional house boat provides indoor shelter. Berlin's summer season starts here.

Der Freischwimmer, Vor dem Schlesischen Tor 2, Kreuzberg
Tel: 6107 4309 www.freischwimmer-berlin.de
Open: 4pm–open-end Mon–Fri; midday–open-end Sat; 11am–open-end Sun

Open 12 months of the year, rain, snow or shine, this pleasant bar can be found on a permanently moored barge. Not the most obvious choice, as the entrance improbably lurks behind a petrol station (oddly enough home to another bar) through an old rusty gate on a pier which also houses water-sports and some allotments. Those that make it down the garden path will find a predominantly eclectic young Kreuzberg crowd, drawn to its laid-back, flea-market decorated living-room vibe. During summer months, drinkers recline on the outside decks, often as a prelude to the Club der Visionäre located opposite, but when the weather turns cold they retreat inside to huddle in front of a log fire in the cosy cabin on deck. A basic menu of fish and chips and other snacks is available, but its all about the location with Freischwimmer.

FC Magnet, Veteranenstraße 26, Prenzlauer Berg
Tel: 4435 2218 www.fcmagnet.de
Open: 8pm–open-end daily

A blip on Germany's otherwise sparkling football reputation, Berlin's local team is a triumph of optimism over reality. But that doesn't seem to bother regulars at this football fanatics' drinking-hole. At weekends crowds gather for a game of *kicker* (table football) overshadowed by a giant picture of Franz

Beckenbauer. Players take themselves very seriously (no spinning, please), and the bar even boasts its own team. Surprisingly, there's not a beer-swilling hooligan in sight; instead a crowd of beautiful people frequent, in outfits so striking they could score a hat trick, and with impeccably angular haircuts probably fashioned with a setsquare. Blaring electro-house music pumps through speakers at the weekends when the bar is at its busiest. If a Berlin bar were to open in Hoxton, it would be exactly like this. Swallow with a heavy dose of irony.

Fluido, Christburger Straße 6, Prenzlauer Berg
Tel: 4404 3902 www.bar-fluido.de
Open: 8pm–2am Sun–Thurs; 8pm–4am Fri, Sat

The only worthwhile cocktail bar this side of town, Fluido is a real find – although located on an otherwise sleepy street, it's easy to miss. It attracts a young, cool and discerning crowd who come to Fluido to kick back and relax on leather seating below dim red lighting or take up a stool at the sleek long bar. The 180-strong cocktail menu is phenomenal and the team constantly experiment with new creations: Fluido was the first bar in Berlin to offer absinthe cocktails. Newer innovations include a range of low-alcohol *sake* cocktails. With over 80 varieties of rare whisky

and a good selection of beers and spirits imported from all over the world, there's no doubting Fluido as a destination for connoisseurs. The drinks are mixed to perfection.

Gainsbourg – Bar Américain, Savignyplatz 5, Charlottenburg
Tel: 313 7464
Open: 4pm–open-end (summer); 5pm–open-end (winter) daily

Inspired by singer Serge Gainsbourg (who died the year the bar opened), this so-called American bar actually has very little to do with Uncle Sam. Staff, however, insist on shaking their cocktails furiously and will happily (and unusually for Berlin bars) converse in English. Well known (and loved) by locals, the bar is often full

to capacity. Attempting to order a drink can be tricky, as a lively crowd jostles for space in a dimly lit and slightly pokey interior. This isn't the place to come for a quiet drink, so be prepared for the odd spillage or an elbow in your face, but when it comes to kick-starting a party, Gainsbourg at least reliably delivers and amid all the commotion staff still make a damn good cocktail. When weather permits, drinkers in need of fresh air pitch up at one of the outdoor tables.

Gorki Park, Weinbergsweg 25, Mitte
Tel: 448 7286
Open: 9.30am–open-end daily

A safe meeting-point for the undecided, Gorki Park is a halfway house between the clubs of Mitte and bars of Prenzlauer Berg. Owned by the team behind restaurant Pasternak (see Eat) and café/bar Gagarin (see Snack), it follows that a loose Russian theme prevails. The menu boasts a good selection of indigenous Russian snacks, including *blini* and *pierogi*. Tables and chairs have been crammed into the three flock-wallpapered rooms and at busy times even a trip to the loo can require some negotiation. The crowd is diverse; students revel in the slightly shabby interior, while scenesters like to pass through on their way to more exclusive spots. In terms of atmosphere, however, Gorki Park is a lively and reliable choice.

Green Door, Winterfeldstraße 50, Schöneberg
Tel: 215 2515 www.greendoor.de
Open: 6pm–3am daily

Glimpsed from the outside, sun-scorched net curtains and a chipped china ornament give the impression Green Door has passed its prime, but step inside and you'll quickly realize why this is one of Berlin's premier cocktail spots. A modern take on the classic drawing room, the interior is bright and trendy – a mixture of picnic-cloth checks and swirling bark etchings. Scriptwriter Fritz Müller-Scherz opened Green Door 14 years ago on the former site of Berlin's legendary Havana Club (the original humidor still exists) and it has thrived ever since. Look out for an unlikely mélange of decorative oddities donated by his aunt, notably the bar's unofficial mascot, a large illuminated dog, the telephone-cum-lamp-cum-cigar-lighter and the battery-powered cocktail shaker, referred to as the oldest barman in

Berlin. Cocktails are a mixture of classic and own-creation, with specials offered every month. House favourite 'The Green Door Cocktail' is a mixture of lemon, sugar, fresh mint and champagne. Happy hour falls between 6pm and 9pm, although the bar is busiest between 9pm and 2am. Classic comfort.

Greenwich Bar, Gipsstraße 5, Mitte.
Tel: None
Open: 8pm–6am daily

Redolent of downtown New York, this über-cool cocktail bar ticks a lot of boxes for Berlin's *jeunesse dorée*. The style-savvy interior, lime-green throughout with tropical fish tanks lining the walls, is a regular in design magazines and the bar has a glamorous, metropolitan vibe. Greenwich is managed by the team behind successful nightlife institution Cookies (currently in

search of a new venue) and exudes a similarly 'too cool for school' attitude. But the mood is friendly and far less self-consciously trendy than other bars in Mitte – look stylish and you'll be embraced as one of their own. Unlike many Berlin cocktail bars, the crowd is casual and most dress down to dress up. T-shirt-clad bar staff successfully keep their cool, even during busy periods. Young and happening; (a good) time starts here.

Hackbath's, Auguststraße 49a, Mitte
Tel: 282 7706 www.hackbaths.de
Open: 9am–open-end daily

Once a bakery in GDR times, this charming building actually dates back to the 1800s and a sense of wistful nostalgia still hangs heavily in the air. Tucked along a quiet street, it's a peaceful spot for a couple of drinks in really comfortable surroundings. If you want to hear yourself think, this is the place. During the day breakfasts and coffees are served and an artsy, creative crowd of

late-risers drop by to read the paper. Early evening, the post-work crowd descends to unwind over a few drinks with light-hearted conversation. A gold-plated and marble-topped bar cuts into the room like a ship's helm, while deep blue tiles offset a classic vintage look. Cocktails are served along with beers on tap. Occasionally owners like to make obscure political statements; during the US presidential elections a glass cabinet was inexplicably filled with tins of Heinz baked beans.

KMA Bar, Karl-Marx-Allee 36, Friedrichshain
Tel: None
Open: 6.30pm–open-end. Closed Sundays.

There's the possibility Big Brother really could be watching you
in this 'glass box' bar on the former Stalin Allee. One of several
impressive examples of GDR architecture in this area, the giant
transparent cube was once a cosmetic studio. Revamped by the
owners of underground club Lovelite, the KMA is now one of
the trendiest bars in town. Although a distance from the main
drag, it's a useful spot for visitors to the Kino International cinema opposite and occasional club venue Café Moskao.
Downstairs, guests relax in full view of the street, while a parti-
tioned mezzanine level offers greater privacy. DJs regularly spin a
selection of cutting-edge sounds from lounge through to electro.
The bar has no name or street number, but a definite identity.
Impossible to miss.

Kumpelnest 3000, Lützostraße 23, Tiergarten
Tel: 261 6918 www.kumpelnest3000.com
Open: 5pm–5am daily (open-end Fri, Sat)

It's well known among Berliners that this quirky shoe-box-sized
bar is strictly for 'the last drink of the night' – principally because
after a few cocktails the garish shag pile carpet and mirrored
walls blur into one confusing mass of colour. Long-time barman
Reinhardt has taken it on himself to decorate the place in his

'downtime'. His latest additions include a ceiling decorated with photocopies of Peter Pan rugs and a home-made mobile of a naked man floating through different household scenes (the backdrop changes each week). There's a photo of an old woman above the bar whom Reinhardt jokingly refers to as his boss. Having opened 18 years ago, Kumpelnest has witnessed a great deal of change. In the early post-Reunification days, the bar would regularly stay open well into the following afternoon. These days it tends to close at 5am in the week and 10am at weekends. Turn up early for sedate music and late if you like it banging.

Neue Bohnen, Schlesische Straße 28, Kreuzberg
Tel: 4703 2236 www.neuebohnen.de
Open: 11am (midday Sat)–1am. Closed Sundays.

When Neue Bohnen threw an opening party 18 months ago, the night ended not in disarray, but with five consecutive games of chess. An obsession with the game continues and several chess tables and chess clocks can be found inside the bar. Occasionally, international tournaments also take place. But game-playing is not the only pastime for guests at Neue Bohnen; musicians from the Gorki theatre often drop by for an improvised jazz session while experimental electronic music events sometimes take place. During the week a €4 lunch deal is also popular. There's a genuine sense of community about Neue Bohnen and a belief that, creatively, anything's possible.

Newton Bar, Charlottenstraße 57, Mitte
Tel: 2061 2999 www.newton-bar.de
Open: 10am–open-end daily

The legendary German photographer lends both his name and photographs to this classy mid-town bar, and the famous stiletto-heeled nudes provide ample distraction for the many tourists who come to gawp. Conveniently located over the road from restaurant Lutter und Wegner (see Eat) (who actually opened Newton in 1999), it's also a popular choice for post-dinner drinks. The space is large and finding a table is never difficult, but glass windows looking onto the busy Gendarmenmarkt can make guests feel slightly exposed to prying eyes. Upstairs, a cigar club and smoking room can be hired for private functions. The crowd is largely conservative – mainly diplomats and business-

men – but always sophisticated. The Martini and whisky selection come highly recommended.

Orient Lounge, Oranienstraße 13, Kreuzberg
Tel: 6956 6762
Open: 9am–3am (summer); 4pm–3am (winter) daily

While most of the bars on Oranienstraße cater to heavy-metal moshers and indie kids, the Orient Lounge has higher expectations. A door lady keeps a watchful eye on guests who pass through the beaded curtains into a lounge room on a par with a harem's den. Romantic couples quickly head for secluded corners, while larger groups find comfort in a fully cushioned room. Inspired by Moorish architecture, light twinkles through star-shaped wall carvings as guests relax with cocktails, teas and water pipes. Despite the door policy, there's no real dress code (this is Berlin!) and the crowd is mainly young and casual. Food is served at downstairs bar Rote Harfe, which was once a popular Irish pub.

San Remo Upflamör, Falkensteinstraße 46, Kreuzberg
Tel: 6128 6795 www.sanremo-upflamoer.de
Open: midday (Fri/Sat 10am)–open-end daily.

A trend-friendly hang-out situated below 'the curve' of the S-Bahn tracks. This area was once a borderline between East and

West Germany and the division lingers on: an annual water-fight still takes place on the Oberbaumbrücke (bridge) between rival residents of Friedrichshain and Kreuzberg. The bar is one of several in the area, but remains the most popular. The owners, who both hail from the small village of Upflamör in south Germany, insist on a non-design ethic, with retro furnishings purchased from flea markets and junk stores and a trendy crowd of boho creatives seem to love the haphazard stylings. Coffee and cakes are served during the day along with a light menu of home-made soups and snacks. Outside tables are also busy on a warm day. Good choice for a drink before visiting the nearby Watergate club.

Sanatorium 23, Frankfurter Allee 23, Friedrichshain
Tel: 4202 1193 www.sanatorium23.de
Open: 11am–open-end daily

The owners of Sanatorium like to think of it as a wellness centre for those sick of reality; on a Friday night, it could be mistaken as a clinic for the mentally insane (when the bar occasionally closes at 8am). It's an environment that fits perfectly with this peculiar stretch of the Karl-Marx-Allee. A hospital theme pervades, with latex surgeon suits hanging from the ceiling and several curtained operating areas. Even the cocktail menu corresponds to the periodic table (which can also be downloaded from the website). Thankfully, the atmosphere isn't quite so sanitized, although the music can be loud and electronic. Strangely enough, Sanatorium is a peaceful choice for a relaxing daytime coffee – although we wouldn't recommend you try the food. Owners Stefan and Anja are also planning to open a small guesthouse above the bar – at present only three double rooms costing €35–45 a night. Each will be designed differently, but along similar lines to the bar. Somebody pass the morphine!

Scotch and Sofa, Kollwitzstraße 18, Prenzlauer Berg
Tel: 4404 2371
Open: 3pm–open-end daily

It's not hard to find Scotch and Sofa; just head for the large flashing neon light installation (depicting a leaping monkey and naked men frog-marching), which dominates the outside wall. Step inside the net curtained doorway and you could be paying a visit to your grandparents – were it not for the selection of whisky

bottles behind the bar. The flock wallpaper, velour lampshades and framed family portraits are textbook '50s prefab. Only a briefcase-carrying businessman cooing 'Honey, I'm home' could complete the look. Even more random furnishings litter the downstairs area, illuminated only by dim red light; a sofa can be found on a fur-covered windowsill with a broken TV set looming ominously in the corner. Bar service can be frosty, but that doesn't deter the crowds which are young, mixed and comfortably clear of the cutting edge. Sunday is Elvis night.

Universum Lounge, Kurfürstenstraße 153, Wilmersdorf
Tel: 8906 4995 www.universumlounge.com
Open: 6pm–3am (4am Fri/Sat) daily

Part of the famous Schaubühne, this space-age cocktail bar attracts a crowd beyond that of regular theatre-goers. Originally built as a cinema in 1927, the building was designed by Mandelson and is a fine example of Bauhaus architecture. The bar borrows its name from the cinema, which has in turn inspired the intergalactic theme. Designed by German firm Player and Franz, playful seating vaguely hints at an astronaut's suit while planetary images abound. The bar offers a range of classic and unique cocktails and guests are encouraged to experiment, especially since happy-hour prices run from 6 to 9pm daily. Universum specializes in Martinis – try the espresso Martini for a caffeine hit or the beautifully crafted apple Martini. As you'd expect of a West Berlin venue, the crowd is suitably flash and

entrance for non-theatre goers is possible only with a code, accessed by logging onto the website. In the summer tables are set outside, and in the absence of any residential noise restrictions, the party often stretches well into the night.

Victoria Bar, Potsdamer Straße 102, Tiergarten
Tel: 2575 9977 www.victoriabar.de
Open: 6pm–open-end daily

According to gourmet German guide *Marcellino's*, this is the best cocktail bar in Berlin. It's certainly one of the most popular and a general leveller for connoisseurs of all types and tastes. Designer Kalle Ingo Strobel and painter Thomas Hauser are responsible for the impressive interior, a mixture of dark wood tones and retro styling. Every aspect of its furnishing has been chosen with care, making Victoria as much a scene as a place to be seen. As you'd expect, the fashionable and wealthy clientele arrive in attire fitting to their surroundings and an unspoken door policy does exist. During busy times every seat at the long and sleek bar is taken – and that's no surprise given the calibre of cocktail mixing. An oasis of style in an otherwise unremarkable area, this is the place to join the jet set.

Weinerei, Veteranenstraße 14, Mitte
Tel: 440 6983 www.weinerei.com
Open: 8pm–midnight daily

A wine bar with a social conscience, the Weinerei collective is a breath of fresh air on the Berlin bar scene. Just like Naomi Klein's classic book there is 'no logo' outside this bar and, very much in the spirit of her ethics, this is an egalitarian enterprise. Inside, there's no bar as such – just a table littered with wine bottles. Guests are invited to pour their own drinks and payment is discretionary. In the absence of any cash register, drinkers simply toss coins into a glass bowl. There are no set prices, but as a rough guide we recommend €3 for a glass of wine. A simple three-course meal is also served from 8pm (again,

pay for as much as you've had) and for breakfast a selection of pastries can be nibbled. It's a concept that relies wholly on trust, but one that has been extremely successful and there are several other branches of Weinerei (Grunli at Strelitzerstraße 56, open: Wed, Fri from 8pm; Loch at Kollwitzstraße 41, open: daily from 8pm). A living-room interior has been cobbled together from flea market finds and one room even resembles an old-fashioned train carriage. Only friends of the Weinerei are welcome, although in truth the offer of friendship extends to everyone. Note the early-for-Berlin closing times!

White Trash, Torstraße 201, Mitte
Tel: 0179 473 2639 www.whitetrashfastfood.com
Open: 6pm–open-end daily

If irony is the new fashion, then White Trash is this season's 'must have'. Set up by two American hobos in a disused Chinese restaurant, White Trash quickly established itself by word of mouth as one of the coolest joints in town. The service sucks (in a nice way) and the food is pure junk (try the Elvis Burger), but cool Berliners and ex-pats are still eager to hang out until the early hours. Cocktails are served and guests can choose between either 'expensive' or 'shit' spirits. Occasionally, bands play live and rock stars visiting Berlin often cruise through the lantern-lit doorways. At peak times the whole room heaves and sweat drips from the ceiling. Paraphernalia of all junky sorts litters the two

rooms – from tropical fish tanks to disembodied plastic limbs – all for sale at the right price. The real fun begins in the twilight hours of 3 until 5am when drunken revellers have been known to dance on tables with their pants on their heads. Essentially a members' club, but if staff like the look of you they'll let you in. Crap has never been so cool.

Windhorst, Dorotheenstraße 65, Mitte
Tel: 2045 0070
Open: 6pm–open-end Mon–Fri; 9pm–open-end Sat, Sun

Despite its close proximity to the US Embassy, this small but classic cocktail bar is not over-run by diplomats. On the contrary, Windhorst attracts a crowd of friendly regulars more than happy to engage in conversation. The fact that owner Günter Windhorst also works behind the bar makes the service even more personal. Having trained as a barman in Kreuzberg institu-

tion Würgeengel, he embarked on his own enterprise five years
ago. Located almost in the centre of town, it's an ideal stop for
theatre-goers and visitors to Berlin's opera house. Paintings of
jazz greats provide the only decoration in an otherwise plain
interior – a hint at the owner's preferred music choice. A great
atmosphere in great company – whether you arrive with some-
one or not.

Wohnzimmer, Lettestraße 6, Prenzlauer Berg
Tel: 445 5458   www.wohnzimmer.de
Open: 10am–4am daily

This 'living-room'-style bar evokes the spirit of post-Wall Berlin
in the days when squat parties would last for weeks. When
Reindol Klenner first opened the bar seven years ago, he had
just one main room. In time, extensions have been made and
Wohnzimmer is now quite literally a 'full house'. A fully fitted
kitchen features a refrigerator, Welsh dresser, carving knife – in
fact, everything including the kitchen sink. Other items of furniture were acquired from flea markets, theatres and even a castle,
and it's quite probable that beneath the tobacco stains many are
valuable antiques. In particular look out for the *verlobungssofa* – a
double-sided courtship chair where never the knee will meet.
The building dates back to 1900 and has always been a traditional German *Eck kneipe* (pub); the wooden bar fittings were added
in GDR times. During the day coffees and light breakfasts are
served, but the interior can feel somewhat gloomy. The cool

crowd descend after dark and sofa surf into the early hours. The
ultimate house party.

Würgeengel, Dresdener Straße 122, Kreuzberg
Tel: 615 5560 www.wuergeengel.de
Open: 7pm–open-end daily

Enchanting even from the outside, Würgeengel is a quintessen-
tially charming bar. On a summer's evening an outdoor bench,
shielded only by creeping ivy and moonlight, is a romantic spot
for a glass of vintage wine or a fine whisky. Inside, plush red
booths and small wooden tables are classic 1930s. Crystal lamps
and candles provide the only light – and are perfect for conspiratorial conversation. The bar is particularly famous for its whisky
selection and high standard of professionalism among staff. Many
of the city's top barmen picked up their tricks by mixing here. A

middle-aged crowd of respectable guests frequent, often after a meal in the neighbouring 'Gorganzola Club' where slightly above-average Italian food is served. Tip: if you're feeling the cold, you can get from one to the other via a secret passageway.

Zebrano, Sonntagstraße 8, Friedrichshain
Tel: 2936 5874 www.zebranobar.de
Open: 10am–open-end daily

This cool and instantly likeable bar takes its name from the exotic African wood used to make the DJ booth and many of the other furnishings. A cosmopolitan crowd of artists, students and locals regularly gather for a relaxed drink and finger food. Retro furnishings from every decade make up a minimalist but comfortable interior and several TV screens above the bar show cartoons, short films or animal documentaries. These idiosyncratic touches appeal to a light-hearted and good-humoured crowd. Art house film screenings take place regularly and DJs spin a selection of broken beat, reggae and nu-soul. Young, fun and very personable, Zebrano makes for perfect lounging.

snack...

In Berlin, the distinction between café, bar and even restaurant is wonderfully loose. Coffee machines switch to optics and beer pumps over the course of a day and light snacks are always served. Owing to low rents and an abundance of empty space, much of the city's café scene is focused in the East. More classic and old-fashioned coffee houses such as Café Savigny, Einstein and the Wintergarten are located in the West.

Breakfast is big business in Berlin and is often served until 4pm – a reflection of the creative community who keep irregular working hours. The best breakfasts are served at Tomasa and Sowohlsoauch. A variety of dishes is served, from cold cuts and cheese to champagne and caviar. At the weekends, most cafés switch to a buffet brunch for a set price. Café im Nu and November are particularly good.

Another German tradition is that of afternoon *Kaffee und Kuchen* (coffee and cakes). Tasty home-made cakes and pastries are available at most places. Find the best home-made selections at Sowohlsoauch, Café im Nu and Café Savigny. Another good source of sweet snacks is trend-friendly Kauf Dich Glücklich, where waffles and ice cream are the main attraction. The café also functions as a shop for local designers, who hang their wares between furnishings. This dual identity is common of many ventures in Berlin: Fräulein Smilla's is a café/furni-

ture and bookshop and Café Sternstaub is also a performance space. Don't be surprised to find cafés that double as launderettes or even tailor's outlets as you wander through the city.

The coffee in Berlin is of a reliably high standard – usually a mixture of German and Italian blends. Health teas are also popular and several infusions are available. During the cold winter months, a glass of *Glühwein* (mulled wine) proves irresistible and some say even medicinal.

In general, Berliners like to eat on the move and it's impossible to travel far without stumbling on the ubiquitous *Imbiss* (snack) stalls. It might seem strange to us, but it's not uncommon for locals to grab a quick sausage on the way home from work. Turkish kebab shops have flooded the Kreuzberg area (mostly pretty good); contrary to urban myth, the donar kebab was actually invented in Berlin.

A strong café culture has evolved in several pockets of the city. The leafy streets around Prenzlauer Berg are popular with a strolling Sunday crowd of young middle-class families. Gagarin and Anita Wrongski both overlook the stunning Wasserturm (water tower) on Kollwitzplatz. Both Kastanianallee (Schwarz-Sauer, Morganrot) and Helmholzplatz (Kakoa) have a younger, more fashionable atmosphere. If in Kreuzberg, head for Bermanstraße, the Paul-Linke-Ufer or – if in search of a more alternative vibe – the Oranienstraße.

Many cafés are worth a visit simply for their location. The Tadschikische Teestube is a magnificent piece of cultural history, Van Loon was once a Dutch sailing boat and Café Bravo is quite literally a piece of art. Berliners also make good use of their green areas and the park cafés are wonderful for lounging on a warm summer's afternoon; try Café Schönbrunn or Schleusenkrug.

Anita Wrongski, Knaackstraße 26, Prenzlauer Berg
Tel: 442 8483
Open: 9am–2am Mon–Sat; 10am–2am Sun

A landmark on the local café map, Anita Wrongski is a popular
choice with the many artists and actors living in Prenzlauer Berg.
Casual mid-morning meetings take place over the simple wood-

en furnishings and a mezzanine level offers seclusion and comfort when in the company of a good book. Large prints of nostalgic black-and-white photographs fill the wall space and tall iron
radiators climb from floor to ceiling. During the week, the space
offers a peaceful sanctuary for roaming free-thinkers, with only
the irresistible spluttering of a coffee machine offering any inter-
ruption. At weekends, however, young families descend and the
ground-floor space can become an assault course of prams and
pushchairs. Outdoor tables affording a view of the Wasserturm
(water tower) are consistently busy, since of all the cafés in this
area Anita Wrongski receives the most sunshine. During the
week an ambitious menu of à la carte breakfast dishes is served
and on Sundays guests can expect a generous buffet, with an
emphasis on fresh and healthy ingredients. Comfortably bohemian.

Ankerklause, Kottbusser Damm 104, Kreuzberg
Tel: 693 5649 www.ankerklause.de
Mon 10am–4pm Mon; 10am–open-end Tues–Sun

This canal-side café is always busy – particularly when Berlin's bi-weekly Turkish market takes over the waterways. Something of a local institution, it's certainly unique, and perfectly suited to the alternative Kreuzberg crowd. Taking the seafaring theme to the extreme, the interior is awash with neon plastic fish and under-water paraphernalia. Diner-style booths are popular with students and can be smoky; venture deeper in for more pleasant seating overlooking the water. Breakfast is served until 4pm, with snacks until 11pm. At night, the disco ball is used to full effect and the well-stocked jukebox attracts a rock'n'roll crowd every Thursday. Thankfully sea shanties are not on the selection!

April, Winterfeldstraße 56, Schöneberg
Tel: 216 8869 www.restaurant-april-berlin.de
Open: 10am–midnight daily

Although there are many cafés in up-and-coming Schöneberg, very few are worthy of a mention. April is arguably the best spot, offering an interesting menu in comfortable surroundings. Close to the Winterfeldplatz, it's the perfect pit-stop for bargain hunters scouting the Saturday-morning antiques market. The breakfast platters (ranging from traditional to ambitious) come highly recommended, each prepared with a touch of the gour-met. The walls are filled with framed film posters while silver cherubs hang above the bar. During the week, April is a popular lunchtime choice for the business crowd, and it also functions as a restaurant well into the night; stone-oven-baked pizzas and *flammkuchen* (a flat savoury bread) are especially popular. Staff can be a little brusque and are often more preoccupied with their own social life than taking your order.

Barcomi's Deli, Sophienstraße 21, Sophie-Gips-Höfe, 2 Hof, Mitte
Tel: 2859 8363   www.barcomi.de
Open: 9am (10am Sun)–10pm daily

Situated in a courtyard below the Sammlung Hoffman gallery (a private collection of modern art), this popular New York-style deli has a good local reputation. A choice of 13 house coffee blends is available, with all beans roasted at Barcomi's smaller mother branch on Bergmannstraße in Kreuzberg (worth a visit to see the giant roasting machine displayed in the shop window).

Delicious New York cheesecakes, muffins and chocolate cakes
are also freshly baked daily (also at the Kreuzberg premises).
There's no breakfast menu as such, but a selection of toasts and
bagels are enough to keep the appetite satiated. Although popular with the media set, the Mitte location lacks the charm and
intimacy of its Kreuzberg counterpart.

Bateau Ivre, Oranienstraße 18, Kreuzberg
Tel: 6140 3659
Open: 9am–3am daily

Too large to be termed a drinking den, but with the appropriate
conspiratorial atmosphere, Bateau Ivre is a local landmark on the
busy Oranienstraße. The space has a weathered and warmly
inviting feel, befitting the alternative crowd of intellectuals and
free-thinkers who frequent it. The café takes its name from a
poem by Rimbaud, which can be found printed along one of the

back walls. Colourful paper lanterns bob gently on ropes suspended from the ceiling, giving the appearance of bizarrely oversized bunting. By mid-morning a blanket of cigarette smoke and
steam from the bar-top coffee machine shrouds the room, making Bateau Ivre a halfway house between café and local pub.
Fortunately, light relief comes in the form of floor-to-ceiling windows, which surround the building. A secluded mezzanine level is
the perfect place to people-watch.

Café am Engelbecken, Michaelkirchplatz, Kreuzberg
Tel: none
Open: 10am–midnight daily

Tranquil spots are often hard to come by in a city centre, but this charming lakeside café is definitely an exception. Once a site for storage containers, the Café am Engelbecken can be found at the bottom of a water-filled quarry. The young owners have certainly achieved success in transforming this once lifeless shell into a stylish and serene environment. A sizeable outdoors terrace provides the biggest draw, enjoying sunlight from dawn til dusk. In the company of only nesting swans, the café feels wonderfully removed from the rest of civilization. And if it happens to rain, the modern but soft furnished interior offers an adequate retreat. Enjoy coffees, cocktails and Asian-inspired dishes.

Café Bravo, Auguststraße 69, Mitte
Tel: 2759 4067
Open: 10am–1am daily

Part of the famous Kunst-Werke Berlin Gallery (a space that has strong links with New York's Museum of Modern Art), this unique café can easily be missed from the street. Lying inconspicuously at the back of a courtyard and hop garden, the café was originally designed by Dan Graham as a piece of art; Bravo is now a favoured haunt for artists and design students. Made entirely of steel and glass, the cube-shaped building fills with light on a sunny afternoon. During summer months Bravo also hosts a number of parties and theatre performances, and DJs often play well into the night. Revellers can recline at one of the many tables or inside Pedro Reyes's remarkable Copolo – two con-

nected spheres fashioned from woven rope and plastic. A selection of light snacks and fruit shakes are served, all using fresh and healthy ingredients. A real find.

Café Einstein, Kurfürstenstraße 58, Tiergarten
Tel: 261 5096 www.cafeeinstein.com
Open: 9am–12am daily

A Berlin institution, this classic Vienna coffee house has spawned its own high-street chain, but this particular branch retains its

traditional character and waiting staff. Albeit a little stuffy, Einstein is a piece of living history. Along with a connoisseur coffee and cake selection, light dishes (including a legendary *Wiener schnitzel*) are also served. Staff are formal but always friendly and attentive. From opening to close, Einstein enjoys a steady turnover and table reservations are recommended for lunch. A constant hustle brings life to the building, but this still isn't the spot to sit back and savour a quiet cup of tea. Inevitably, tourists frequently descend on Einstein, but it continues to be a favourite with locals who enjoy a sweet taste of the high life.

Café Bistro im Nu, Lychener Straße 41, Prenzlauer Berg
Tel: 4471 8898
Open: 8am–10pm daily. (longer hours in summer)

Once considered a no-go zone during the early reunification days, the Helmholzplatz is now a bustling hub of trendy bars and cafés. Of all those on offer, Café Bistro im Nu offers arguably the best home-baked food. The mouth-watering cakes are made by owner Adrianne on the premises and the mixed berry cheesecake is definitely not to be missed. Sunday's buffet brunch is served until 4pm and includes a generous selection of tasty dishes and home-made breads served fresh from the oven. Juices and yoghurt shakes are a healthy alternative to the more traditional *Kaffee und Kuchen*. The interior is awash with pastel colours and art-deco decoration, while plush red window seating is a popular choice on a sunny day, when the café is otherwise left a little in

the shade. The crowd is refreshingly mixed and less self-consciously trendy than other nearby hang-outs. Friendly and familiar, like a warm hug from grandma.

Café November, Husemannstraße 15 Prenzlauer Berg
Tel: 442 8425 www.november-café.de
Open: 9am–2am daily (kitchen closes at 11.30)

One of the oldest cafés in Prenzlauer Berg, November has
weathered a storm of short-lived enterprises in this area.
Formerly a fishmonger's, the café opened in its current incarnation back in 1989 as part of the reconstruction of Husseman
Straße, and in terms of both décor and clientele little has
changed since. In a district where businesses are characteristic-
ly in flux, November owes its longevity to its favour with locals
as a reliable and safe bet. At weekends, the sturdy wooden tables
are littered with magazines and copies of *Der Spiegel*. Sundays are

particularly busy, when couples flock to savour the highly recommended buffet brunch served until 6pm. Intriguingly, guests are
even invited to make their own waffles. On a good day, light spills
through the large glass windows and seating is also available outside. At night candlelight gently illuminates the dark brown interi-
or as the evening meals are served; it's the perfect setting to sink
a bottle or two of red wine. November classes itself as a gay
café, but the crowd is largely mixed. Relaxing and spacious.

Café Savigny, Grolmanstraße 53, Charlottenburg
Tel: 3151 9612
Open: 9am–1am daily

One of the few dedicated cafés in this area, Café Savigny has
been serving customers for the last 24 years. Exuding all the
atmosphere of a traditional Viennese coffee house with waiters
dressed in formal attire, the more modern laid-back surroundings and cosmopolitan touches (such as the supply of foreign

newspapers) fix Savigny firmly in its 20th-century context. Faux-
Roman friezes decorate the otherwise simple interior and an
ornate chandelier is a reminder that customers are in an exclusive area of Berlin. A selection of high-quality home cooking
graces the daily menu; of particular note is the *1001 Nacht
Frühstuck* (56g Russian caviar, smoked salmon and a bottle of
Krug). All sandwiches are served with a knife and fork – another
sign of the 'comfort meets high-class' maxim on which Savigny
thrives. The place is particularly well known for it's small but
delicious selection of home-made cakes. As its a popular shopping pit-stop with ladies-who-lunch, the larger tables are often
reserved.

**Café Schönbrunn, Im Volkspark Friedrichshain,
Friedrichshain**
Tel: 4679 3893
Open: 10am–1am daily

A little off the beaten track, this elevated park café is well worth the trek on a summer's day. Floor-to-ceiling windows fill the space with light and give fantastic views of the park's swan lake and Japanese garden. The '70s-styled interior betrays the café's fledgling four years. As night falls cocktails are served at the James-Bond-style bar, lined with bulbous white bar stools. During summer months, crowds spill onto the large veranda outside where snacks are served from a kiosk and DJs spin the decks, especially during the Love Parade. The vibe is young and effortlessly cool. New ownership has put an end to any grand party plans and there are now attempts to take Schönbrunn upmarket as a restaurant – but as yet these have met with little success. Look out for the fairy-tale fountain and socialist realist art elsewhere in the park. Tricky to find in the dark!

Café Sternstaub, Gneiststraße 10, Prenzlauer Berg
Tel: 9599 8068
Open: 11am–open-end. Closed Mondays.

An assortment of treasures and theatrical props fills this pleasant café-cum-performance space. A white feather plume hangs gracefully above the bar, while seating ranges from an antique embroidered chaise longue to deck chairs that wouldn't look out of place in Margate. The interior is admittedly eclectic, but a cut above the archetypal ramshackle Berlin café. Close to the trendy Helmholzplatz, Sternstaub provides a quiet retreat from the madding Sunday afternoon crowds. An ideal spot to catch the afternoon sun, tables and chairs are often dragged onto the pavement outside. A limited breakfast menu is offered until 5pm and on afternoons a choice of three home-made cakes from the French patisserie is available. Evenings are given over to the experimental arts; plays, poetry readings and musical events attract a suitably dramatic crowd. Instantly inclusive, it's easy to find a soft spot for Sternstaub.

Café Wintergarten im Literaturhaus, Fasanenstraße 23, Charlottenburg
Tel: 882 5414 www.literaturhaus-berlin.de
Open: 9.30–1am daily

Those in search of a quiet retreat from the marauding shoppers of Ku'damm should head for the conservatory café of West Berlin's Literaturhaus. Built in 1886, the wrought-iron building was initially for domestic use; a hundred years later it became a home to writers and literary forums. Elderly couples and stylish women sit down to enjoy their afternoon coffee and cake with a silver service. But unlike many of the traditional coffee houses in Berlin, the Wintergarten has a modern feel. During summer guests kick back with a traditional Berlin white beer and a slice of raspberry tart on one of the large garden benches, while during the winter months they gaze at the frosty lawns from the warmth and comfort indoors. An impressive selection of international newspapers is available and there is a bookshop downstairs. Guaranteed to banish even the most stubborn writer's block.

Cream, Schlesische Straße 6, Kreuzberg
Tel: 6107 4980
Open: 8am–9pm Mon–Sat; 9am–9pm Sun

If caffeine is your vice, then Cream could represent a dangerously dark underworld. From Ethiopian to Cuban, Bolivian to African – the choice of coffee blends is overwhelming. In a place where 'instant' is a dirty word, every effort has been made to ensure cups are filled with liquid gold. All the beans are imported fresh and roasted locally, and the smell wafting from the percolators is alone enough to seduce the senses. Further sustenance comes in the form of an excellent breakfast menu and a selection of freshly baked muffins and cakes. The space is clean-cut and modern, which seems to attract the local professionals. Meticulous atten-

tion to detail gives the impression that Cream belongs to a chain
– but then maybe that's all part of the connoisseur treatment.

Ehrenburg, Karl-Marx-Allee 103A, Friedrichshain
Tel: 4210 5810
Open: 10am–open-end daily

When cafés first opened on this once-isolated stretch, propri-
etors would lock their doors after every customer for fear of
what might happen. Now, the imposing Karl Marx Allee is an up-
and-coming area, with a growing collection of new cafés, bars
and restaurants. Named after the Russian Communist intellectual
Ehrenburg, this curious coffee stop is an unrivalled spot for
thoughtful contemplation. Originally an East German paper shop,
Ehrenburg was renovated in keeping with Stalinist sentiments of
grandeur by its artistically minded owners. A giant square-shaped
bar forms the focal point, and decoration is kept to a clutter-free
minimum. By day, light spills through the giant square windows
and at night the space is filled with a strangely surreal but allur-
ing orange light. Incidental music, a mixture of cult movie classics
and '30s jazz, adds to the askew experience.

Fräulein Smilla's, Pappelallee 63, Prenzlauer Berg
Tel: None   www.frauleinsmillas.de
Open 9.30am–8pm Mon–Fri; 11am–6pm Sat; times vary Sun

More than just a coffee shop, Fräulein Smilla's has been a labour of love for friendly owners Annette and Joe. A bookshop, art space, furniture shop and café in one, this fledgling venture already boasts a loyal clientele. Annette is herself a passionate fan of literature and the name 'Fräulein Smilla's' is borrowed from Peter Hoeg's classic novel. A fascinating selection of

second-hand books – ranging from children's to adult – can be found stacked on shelves in a mock living room, complete with quirky fireplace and fur rug. Furnishings are an intriguing mixture of '50s, '60s and '70s design, and available for purchase if so desired. Occasionally art exhibitions and special events are held and book readings take place fortnightly on a Sunday; light snacks and drinks are served, often inspired by the book in question. A unique enterprise, Fräulein Smilla's is definitely worth a visit.

Gagarin, Knaackstraße 22–24, Prenzlauer Berg
Tel: 442 8807 www.bar-gagarin.de
Open: 10am–open-end daily

Paying homage to astronaut Yuri Gagarin, this patriotic café follows an accordingly Soviet theme. Next door to Russian restaurant Pasternak, it forms a pocket of USSR nostalgia in former East Berlin. Red stars and sputniks may be in abundance, but these days there's little political activity. Instead, it's a great spot to sip on Russian vodkas and sup on authentic *Pelminis* and other traditional delicacies. A safe step back from the cutting edge, the crowd is young but not self-consciously trendy. The café enjoys a steady turnover, but very rarely reaches capacity; mid-mornings are busiest, when a hearty breakfast menu draws in a crowd. But be warned about the weekend music policy: after an hour of listening to ear-splitting techno, your eggs won't be the only things that are scrambled!

Joseph Roth Diele, Potsdamer Straße 75, Tiergarten
Tel: 2636 9884 www.josephrothdiele.de
Open: 10am–midnight Mon–Fri. Closed weekends.

A tribute to the late 19th-century Jewish author Joseph Roth Diele, who wrote his book *Radetzkymarsch* in this very neighbourhood, the café is a popular meeting-point for literary types and journalists who work in the area. At lunchtimes JRD is particularly bustling (when the most expensive meal is a mere

€3.95), as it is for after-work drinks. Worth sampling is the 'Stullen', an open sandwich served on German rye bread and stored in a large glass cabinet. The owner, film director Dieter Funk, is responsible for the curious but wonderfully photogenic interior; quotations from Diele's books circumnavigate the bar, fashioned from newspaper tears, while the back wall is filled with photographic slides collected from various flea markets. Weekly events include book readings, jazz recitals and DJ sets courtesy of an antique gramophone.

Kaffee Am Meer, Bergmanstraße 95, Kreuzberg
Tel: 6900 1367
Open: 8am–midnight Sun–Thurs; 8am–(usually) 2am Fri, Sat

A clever play on words, the name of this cosmopolitan and upbeat café/bar is taken from the nearby Mehringdam road. Translated as 'café on the sea', the interior loosely follows a sea-

side theme, but don't expect to find beach huts and Hawaiian cocktails; this place is far more classy. A large mural of the ocean horizon hangs above cushioned seating and gives the space a light and airy feel. Outdoor seating spills onto this busy but charming street, and can be found below a heated canopy during winter months. Frequented by an alternative crowd from the Kreuzberg area, the vibe is cool but casual. Breakfast and toasted snacks are served during the day, but by night cocktails provide the preferred sustenance. A breath of fresh sea air.

Kakao, Dunckerstraße 10, Prenzlauer Berg
Tel: 4403 5653 www.intveld.de
Open: midday–2am daily

A chocolate lover's paradise and calorie counter's worst night-
mare, this café – inspired by all things cocoa-based – could give
Willy Wonka a run for his money. Even the interior is good
enough to eat; chocolate brown and milky-white cushioned wall
panels are covered in a treacle of orange light and leather-seated
booths provide comfort you can melt into. Look up to the ceiling to find an LED-lit world map of choc-producing territories.
Whether you have a sweet tooth or not, this stylish interior is
difficult to resist. Each week a different drink is created using the
gourmet chocolate made on the premises. The speciality dish of
the house is somewhat less conventional: a pastry bizarrely filled
with dark chocolate, beef and chilli. Funnily enough, Kakao is the
only café to offer such a dish and draws a crowd of committed
devotees from far afield; give it a go – you won't be disappointed! The 'Isn't Veld Schokoladen' shop next door stocks over 120
different types of chocolate imported from France and Italy
along with more common house brands. More than a quirky
curiosity shop, Kakao is a professional chocoholic's heaven.

**Kauf Dich Glücklich, Oderberger Straße 44,
Prenzlauer Berg**
Tel: 4435 2182
Open: 1–8pm Mon–Fri; midday–8pm Sat, Sun

You can't buy happiness (as the name of this optimistic café might suggest) but there are plenty of other pleasing items for sale at this perennially hip spot. The brainchild of two sisters schooled in interior design, Kauf Dich Glucklich was launched as a creative space for fledgling artists to sell their wares… with a few tasty nibbles tossed into the equation. Scarves, necklaces, shoes and small toys adorn the walls – all with a *selbst gemacht* (home-made) stamp as well as a reasonable price tag. But it's the tasty selection of filled waffles and ice-cream delights that really pulls in the crowds – young and old. Both kitsch and kooky, it's been an instant hit with Berlin's cool clique. Worth a visit after trawling the nearby Sunday flea market at Mauer Park – where most of the retro furnishings were probably purchased.

Knofi, Bermannstraße 11, Kreuzberg
Tel: 694 5807 www.knofi.de
Open: 6am–8pm Mon–Sat, 8am–8pm Sun

This incredible Aladdin's cave of Turkish baked goods and deli products forms one arm of a triumvirate of enterprises in the local area; a smaller deli can be found on Oranienstraße, while a branch across the road specializes strictly in catering for functions. This more recent venture houses a backroom café, oozing with Middle Eastern promise. Strings of garlic (for which Knofi is a colloquialism), cheeses and cured sausages hang from the ceiling, while a wealth of colourful produce and condiments fill every other available space. Many of the baked goods are delivered daily from France, while huge vats of soup and traditional meat parcels are prepared on the premises. An early opening attracts nattering old ladies, while daytimes are the preserve of a wonderfully mixed crowd.

Morganrot, Kastanienallee 85, Prenzlauer Berg
Tel: 4431 7844 www.oekotopia-berlin.de
Open: 11am–open-end. Closed Mondays.

The spirit of the Red Star rules in this ecologically friendly café/bar/collective. Affiliated to the squat next door, Morganrot now functions as a viable but fair trading business. Regardless of class, race or status, everyone is welcome; the cafe is an open space for political discussion, exploration of intellectual ideas and just plain old relaxation – but don't feel obliged to turn up with a copy of *Das Kapital* under your arm. The colourful interior is a

mixture of sculptures and art works designed by local artists, and makes for interesting eye candy. A tasty vegan-vegetarian buffet breakfast is served every day from 11am, for a wonderfully cheap €3. Only fair trade coffee is sold, a percentage of which is donated to social projects in developing countries. Morganrot is the true antithesis of Starbucks café culture.

Schleusenkrug, Müller-Breslau-Straße, Tiergarten
Tel: 313 9909   www.schleusenkrug.de
Open: 10am–open-end (6pm Nov–Feb) daily

Somewhat secluded at the top end of the Tiergarten, this lock-side café feels a million miles from the hustle and bustle of the Ku'damm. African street traders, students, dog walkers and elderly couples all gather on the tables outside to enjoy the riverside sunshine beneath weeping willows. The interior is a mixture of rustic pub and classic 1970s – the focal point being a bizarre light fitting, which could pass as a prop on the Starship Enterprise. There's a definite sense of institution about Schleusenkrug and change is something that happens slowly. The menu is surprisingly good for a café of this sort.

Schwarz-Sauer, Kastanienallee 13, Prenzlauer Berg
Tel: 448 5633
Open: 8am–open-end daily

Easily the busiest pit-stop on the Kastanianallee (though by no means the best), you'll be hard pushed to find a table at this favourite neighbourhood haunt. Serving customers for 11 years, Schwarz-Sauer was the first bar/café in this street. Many of its original customers still stop by for a morning coffee and the clientele is a bizarre mix of crusty old men and fashion-flaunting hipsters. The tiled interior has remained intact since Day 1 and there is little demand for change. At weekends locals clamber for a seat at the wooden horseshoe bar or at one of the many outdoor tables. Food is basic and fairy unremarkable, with sushi served after 6pm. But Schwarz-Sauer plays its trump card during summer months, when all night openings are a dead cert.

Sowohlsoauch, Kollwitzstraße 88, Prenzlauer Berg
Tel: 442 9311 www.kaffeeundkuchen.de
Open: 8am–2am daily

This local favourite is consistently popular, so you'll have to be fast to bag a table here. Weekend or weekday – there's never a quiet period as Berliners return again and again for the reliably good food and delicious selection of home-made cakes. Coupled with an excellent choice of coffee blends, it's the perfect spot to indulge in Germany's afternoon tradition of *Kaffee und Kuchen*'. Taking the Berlin penchant for a late breakfast to the extreme, a mouth-watering menu of hot and cold plates is served until 11pm. Accordingly, however, prices are slightly above average. As is typical of the area, the place is swarming with young mums and their newborns and it's a wonder the waiting staff don't continually trip over the state-of-the-art buggies. But as the day wears on, a refreshingly diverse crowd drifts through the doorway – from boho students to old-school GDR residents. If space is limited inside, take a pew on one of the benches outdoors where gas heaters and blankets provide ample warmth.

Tadschikische Teestube, Palais am Festungsgraben, Am Festungsgraben, Mitte
Tel: 204 1112
Open: 5pm–midnight Mon–Fri; 3pm–midnight Sat, Sun

This surprise fairy-tale tearoom was a present from the government of Tajikistan to the GDR. The carved columns, fine woven rugs and hanging tapestries were all hand-made and initially exported to Leipzig as part of an exhibition in 1974. The interior was relocated entirely in 1976 to the Palais am Festungsgraben, a

former seat of the Prussian ministers for finance. Today the palace houses several grand ballrooms, which are all available for hire and this wonderfully preserved space is open to the public. In keeping with its heritage, the Teestube is a celebration of Tajik culture serving authentic teas and light snacks; guests are asked to remove their shoes and sit on cushions at low-level tables. Every Monday at 6pm, a visiting story-teller entertains guests with traditional fairy-tales (at present only in German). The Teestube is particularly popular in winter and reservations are advised.

Tiki Heart, Weiner Straße 20, Kreuzberg
Tel: 6107 4701 www.wildatheartberlin.de
Open: 10am–2am daily

This overwhelmingly kitsch café is a south-sea island in the northern hemisphere, where the sun shines 365 days of the year. Hawaiian garlands and straw skirts are optional, although sun-glasses could be required after a particularly indulgent night. Totem polls, Aztec carvings and the odd Elvis photograph hang from walls daubed in the sun-splashed colours of the South Pacific. Customers can either pull up a stool at the beach hut cocktail bar or relax back into a wicker peacock throne at a table. A relatively fledgling venture, Tiki Heart was opened by the owners of rock venue Wild At Heart next door and is often used as a pre-gig hang-out for touring bands. Fans of '50s rock and all things be-bop; their own outlandish dress sense is not

dissimilar to the café's vibrant décor and much of Tiki Heart's success is down to their popularity in the local neighbourhood. The menu selection is equally eclectic and presents a fusion of Mexican, German and American cooking (the 'Biker's Breakfast' being a favourite with regulars). For those who can't bear to leave the experience behind, a downstairs shop is stuffed full of '50s memorabilia. Even by Berlin standards, this place is unique.

Tomasa, Motzstraße 60, Schöneberg
Tel: 213 2345
Open: 8am–1am Mon–Thurs; 8am–2am Fri, Sat. Closed Sundays.

In a city where breakfast is considered the King of all Meals, Tomasa should surely be crowned sovereign of all eating establishments. It's a place of local legend, and Berliners regularly make the pilgrimage to this mecca of brunch specialities. And for good reason: the menu is vast and includes interesting combinations from all over the globe. Where else could you find a quail's

egg sunny side up? Of particular merit are the *mezze*-style platters, large enough to feed two. Ingredients are of the highest quality and each dish is prepared with fine dining expertise. A stone's throw from the pleasant Victoria Platz, outdoor seating is busy on a summer's day. A stylishly modern interior makes it popular with a casually affluent crowd.

Van Loon, Carl-Herz-Ufer 5, Kreuzberg
Tel: 692 6293 www.vanloon.de
Open: 10am–1am daily

The River Spree forms the fabric of Berlin's cityscape and there are more bridges in this landlocked capital than in Venice. Originally built as a goods carrier in 1914, then converted to a houseboat in 1972, Van Loon eventually became a restaurant/café in 1988. The boat takes its name from the famous Dutch boat builder, Nicolaos Van Loon (1775–1840). When weather permits, the open-top deck is a great place to enjoy an impressive breakfast selection (served until 3pm) on this quiet stretch of the river. Summer brunch cruises can also be booked on sister restaurant boat *Phillipa*. During the long winter months, guests seek shelter in the cosy cabin below lit only by wall lamps fashioned from coffee cups. Late night marauders can also enjoy the cheese-board served after 11pm! Successfully resisting the tourist trap mould, Van Loon has the character of a local caf.

Volckswirtschaft, Krossener Straße 17, Friedrichshain
Tel: 2900 4604 www.volckswirtschaft.de
Open: 6pm–open-end Mon–Wed, 1pm–open-end Thurs–Sat, 10am–open-end Sun

A restaurant with café ambience, Volckswirtschaft is a popular hang-out for creative bohemians and students in the

Friedrichshain area. Tables of all shapes and sizes fill the intimate space and make for a convivial atmosphere. There's an emphasis on eco-friendly cooking – only organic meats are used in the simple but tasty dishes – and the portions are generous. The menu changes daily with themed dishes for every night of the week; Tuesday's creative home cooking and Friday's fish are particularly popular. Organic beer Pinkus is also sold. On Sundays vegan and vegetarian brunches are served – perfect sustenance after a trip to the flea market on Boxhagener Platz.

party...

In a city with so much confused history, it's hardly surprising that Berlin has interesting nightlife: anger and frustration can often find expression in a desire to escape reality, if only for a while. A maxim of 'anything goes' has applied throughout Berlin's history – from the heady days of 1920s cabaret to the post-Reunification explosion of techno. In the absence of any licensing laws parties can run well into the following day, as they often did during the early '90s. At one time East Berlin was one big party – reflected by such events as the techno-fest Love Parade. More recently things have begun to calm down, and most clubs tend to peak at 2am and wind up around 7am. However, the reopening of legendary venue Ostgut as Berghain/Panorama Bar has reignited an interest in never-ending parties, with most clubbers choosing to arrive after the break of dawn.

Attempting to grasp and understand Berlin's club scene can be frustrating. Venues come and go, parties relocate and hours are never reliable. On the plus side, this makes for a fascinating puzzle to unravel. Arriving at a disused ware-house in the middle of an industrial estate might seem daunting, but once inside the satisfaction of being part of an in-crowd is overwhelming. Without doubt, Berlin boasts one of Europe's most exciting and vibrant club scenes. All clubs listed here are current at the time of press, but it's advisable to check websites before making a trip. Some venues are listed in magazines such as *Tipp* and *Zitty* (the Berlin equivalents of *Time Out*) along with English title *Ex-Berliner*, but many

prefer to remain 'underground'. Clubbers often rely on a sophisticated email system, which is actually fairly simple to tap into. Just sign up on the club websites.

Those seeking a true underground experience will not be disappointed. Clubs such as Weekend, Berghain and Lovelite evoke the atmosphere of the impromptu squat and warehouse parties for which Berlin is so famous. Many will not let you take in cameras, and exercise a selective door policy. For the most part, they try to deter large groups of tourists. No less cutting-edge but far more accessible are clubs such as Watergate and the 103 Club. More mainstream venues are 90 Grad, Sage and Big Eden.

The music scene in Berlin is predominantly electronic – the city is considered by many to be the birthplace of techno. Once a worldwide phenomenon, techno club Tresor has become a tourist attraction, but at the moment is currently in search of a new location. The sounds (and accompanying fashions) of electro and minimal techno, so lauded by our own style press, can be found blasting from most club speakers. Other styles are, however, well represented. A recent boom in reggae has led to regular events at Geburtstagklub (Mondays) and Hoppetosse with the Yaam crew (Sundays). Party organizers Live Demo take care of all things hip-hop and have a regular Tuesday night slot at Stern Radio. Drum'n'bass nights are held at Watergate and Icon, while R&B and house are played at the more mainstream clubs.

On a practical note, most clubs operate a glass deposit system. You'll be charged extra for each drink and given a token. Return this, along with your empty glass and you'll be given a refund.

90 Grad, Dennewitzstraße 37, Schöneberg
Tel: 2759 6231 www.90grad.de
Open: 7pm–open-end Wed, 11pm–open-end Fri, Sat

'90 Degrees' is so named because of the intensity of the party when this mainstream club reaches full capacity, never more so than during the infamous 'after-work' parties. Despite high-end aspirations, this isn't exactly the 'coolest' spot in town; bouncers reek of expensive aftershave, and 90 Grad proudly boasts Europe's only Dom Perignon lounge complete with giant inflatable champagne bottles. Thankfully, the main room is marginally more tasteful and follows an oriental theme. Accordingly a team of sushi chefs is drafted in for Wednesday's after-work party, when the club opens at 7pm. For many, 90 Grad is a welcome antidote to Berlin's über-trendy clubs and industrial warehouses. The music is mainstream dance/R&B and guests are always well turned out. This one-time underground club was once a car garage, and for several months a large car-carrier stood in the main dance-floor.

103 Club, Falckensteinstraße 47, Kreuzberg
Tel: none www.agentur103.de
Open: 11pm–open-end Fri, Sat

Owned by the same team behind the 103 bar in Prenzlauerberg, this is one of the newer and exciting club openings in Berlin (the doors first swung open in February). The team has a history on the club circuit, their first opening was on Friedrichstrasse 103 – hence the name. Their latest venture is marketed as a post-techno club and, despite a run-down exterior, is far more accessible than most warehouse clubs. Attracting a far broader crowd than the style-conscious 103 bar, the venue has already been granted a seal of approval by Berlin's premier party crowd.

Berghain/Panorama Bar, Am Wriezener Bahnhof, S Ostbahnhof, Friedrichshain
Tel: none www.berghain.de
Open: midnight–open-end Fri,Sat.

Currently THE premier spot to go clubbing in Berlin, this gay/mixed club is packed out every weekend. Queues up to an hour long are not uncommon, even at 7am – when some would argue the club just gets going. It succeeded legendary club Ostgut (which closed with a four-day blow-out several years ago), so expectations were high when it opened. Fortunately, the party-hard legacy lives on, making Berghain a mecca for clubbing hedonists worldwide. Housed within a disused power station in an industrial site just behind the Ostbahnhof train station, the club is notoriously difficult to find, but the mystery only adds to the experience. Inside, an imposing concrete staircase leads to the main club space Berghain; the music here is hard with sweat-drenched dancers vying for floor space. Upstairs, the Panorama Bar makes for fantastic people-watching; pretty young trendsetters can be found deep in conversation with burly tattooed men, while dark corners provide the setting for… well, we can let you imagine. There's a strict no camera policy (even camera phones are confiscated) and the only interior shots in existence were taken by Wolfgang Tillmans. Organizers would argue Berghain is a time and a place never to be re-created. Truly electrifying.

Big Eden, Kurfürstendamm 202, Charlottenburg
Tel: 882 6120 www.big-eden.de
Open: 10pm–open-end Tues–Thurs; 11pm–open-end Fri, Sat

Lightning might never strike twice in the same place, but the laws of probability don't apply in this original '70s disco den, where Grease Lightning strikes every night. In its heyday, Big Eden was the big cheese of West Berlin's club scene. Opened by local playboy Rolf Eden, sex, drugs and rock'n'roll quickly found

their home amid the disco-lit interior. Original retro curves and glitter-inflected furnishings make this a film location favourite. American diner-style booths are perfect for flirting or kicking back with a bottle of bubbly. After a dodgy period during the '90s, Big Eden now offers a sound programme of Latin live bands, funk, lounge and the odd kitsch pop act. On Thursdays, name DJs spin a regular R&B and soul night. If out West, this is the only club to check.

Café Moskau, Karl-Marx-Allee 34 Mitte
Tel: none www.kaleidoskop-berlin.de; www.gmf-berlin.de
Open: check websites for party details.

Originally built as East Berlin's showcase Russian restaurant in the 1960s, Café Moskau was also a premier GDR nightclub. Motifs from the former Soviet Union abound, and with separate rooms named after CCCP protectorate cities Tallinn, Riga and Minsk, the USSR lives on – particularly in the fond memories of East Berliners, many of whom married after meeting here in their youth. Today, Moskau plays host to a range of exhibitions and club events: the Jazzanova Kaleidoskop nights take place here monthly, while collectives such as Live Demo (see www.sternradio-berlin.de) and gay party GMF also use the space. If Moskau's music and club nights are not to your taste it's worth a visit simply to admire the fantastic architecture. Downstairs, a long sleek bar splits the room in two, while silver pillars surround the dance-floor; in the courtyard large cube light

installation dominates the space. An impeccable piece of GDR history.

Geburtstagklub, Am Friedrichshain 33, Prenzlauer Berg
Tel: 4202 1405 www.geburtstagsklub.de
Open: 11pm–open-end Mon, Fri, Sat

Birthdays are at the heart and soul of Geburtstagsklub, so-called because of the papier-mâché birthday cake that sits atop the club's humble entrance. Inspiration for the club, housed in what was once a storage warehouse for the owner's lighting business, was born out of a friend's birthday party there. The celebration is still taken seriously and birthday boys and girls are able to waltz in free. Long-standing reggae night Callaloo Club takes place on a Monday, while the monthly famous gay party 'Irrenhouse' ('mad-house') is not for the easily offended; drag shows and naked dancing are not unusual. The club can be found at the bottom of a scruffy courtyard. Events vary drastically, so choose your party with care!

Icon, Cantianstraße 15, Prenzlauer Berg
Tel: 6128 7545 www.iconberlin.de
Open: 10pm–open-end Sun, Mon; 1pm–open-end Tues–Fri;
11.30pm–open-end Sat

Essentially a sweaty basement, Icon remains a permanent fixture on Berlin's otherwise transient club scene. Hosting various drum'n'bass and hip-hop nights (including a regular spot for London's Ninja Tunes label), the club attracts a mainly student and cosmopolitan crowd. Comprising two brick-walled rooms with low ceilings, the space can feel extremely claustrophobic when full, and moving from one room to another is comparable to passing a camel through the eye of a needle. Sweat drips from the ceilings and anyone wearing glasses should expect some serious condensation. The dress code is casual and no one really makes the effort. Unlike most of the chemically fuelled clubs in Berlin, the choice of poison at Icon is always alcohol. Consequently, this is a popular pick-up joint, with raging hormone levels akin to a school disco. A free-for-all that's fit for all.

Insel, Alt-Treptow 6, Treptow
Tel: 2091 4990 www.insel-berlin.net
Open: 7pm–open-end Wed–Sat; 2–8pm Sun

A club with its own island, Insel is one of the more unique spaces in Berlin. Admittedly a way out of town, it's a pleasant bike ride on a summer's night. The castle-like building (based on a painting of a Scottish convent), which dates back to the 1880s, has undergone various incarnations as restaurant and Communist youth centre before evolving into a club spread over three floors with a fantastic roof terrace overlooking the Spree. In the week, the building is used as a rehearsal space for young bands, and various poetry readings, film showings and comedy events also take place.

Live bands and DJs play on Friday and Saturday nights and the
'Lazy Sunday' afternoon party (ska, reggae, downbeat) perfectly
rounds off the weekend. During the summer, bands take to an
outdoor stage, while a young, artistic crowd lounge on hammocks
above the man-made beach. Parties often extend well into the
next day.

Kaffee Burger, Torstraße 60, Mitte
Tel: 2804 6495 www.kaffeeburger.de
Open: 7pm–open-end daily

More a pub with a dance-floor than an actual club, Kaffee Burger
is a general all-rounder. Recently celebrating its 10th year, the
famous Russian Disco takes place intermittently. Following suit
from Vladimir Kaminer's book of the same name, the party

attracts nostalgic '*Ossies*' and anyone with an interest in kitsch Russian pop. Owner poet Bert Papenfuss maintains his craft with spoken-word poetry jams, and live bands play regularly. Entrance is often free, so it's worth dropping by if you've nothing better to do. Dim red lighting adds convivial warmth and works as a convenient camouflage for the slightly shabby interior. Expect a crowd of all shapes, sizes and age.

Kinzo, Karl-Lieknecht-Straße 11, Mitte
Tel: 2887 3883 www.kinzo-berlin.de
Open: 11pm–open-end Thurs–Sat

A downtown shopping arcade provides the unlikely setting for this intimate basement club. Like all worthwhile places in Berlin, it's difficult to find – this time head for the doorway just behind McDonald's. But don't be put off: the welcome is always warm

once you arrive. Downstairs, giant neon letters spell out 'sexy', but the gesture is very much tongue-in-cheek and it certainly isn't the place for glam divas or meat-market professionals! Table football is set up in the corner and young staff will willingly challenge you to a game. Despite the young, funky and design-friendly interior, regulars aren't afraid to dance their socks off and break into a sweat. Refreshment comes in the form of the 'Kinzo Cooler', an orange cocktail that's become a trademark for the club. Music always comes from the cutting edge, but is never too experimental – mainly electro, house and funk.

Lovelite, Simplonstraße 38–40, Friedrichshain
Tel: none www.lovelite.de
Open: 11pm–open-end Fri, Sat

Judging by its artistic temperament, Lovelite really is the word on
the street. Some of Berlin's best graffiti crews and street artists
come down here to write, hang out and listen to music – mainly
underground hip-hop and electronic. A gallery space houses temporary exhibitions, although unofficial pieces on the outside
gates are worth a visit in themselves. Although an independent
initiative, Lovelite is run with professionalism and artistic flair.
The street-savvy crowd are refreshingly broad-minded and open
to musical persuasion. The interior is simple but slick, and the
vibe always upbeat. Rising above the shackles of hype, Lovelite is
a genuinely cool place to relax and kick back. Idiosyncratic
touches – such as the permanently stoned kiosk vendor who
sells tea and toasties from the back of a camper van – only add
to its charm. Owned by the same team behind the KMA bar.

Magnet, Griefswalder Straße 212–213, Prenzlauer Berg
Tel: 4285 1335 www.magnet-club.de
Open: 9pm–open-end Tues, Fri, Sat; 8pm–open-end Sun

Lying somewhere between pub back room and students' union,
Magnet attracts a similar crowd to Icon. But this is definitely one
of the best places to catch up-and-coming rock acts. After gigs,
DJs always spin in a second room were beaten-up sofas sur-

round a simple wooden dance-floor. A mixture of shoe-gazing students, oversized indie kids and air-guitar extremists consider Magnet to be their local haunt. On Wednesdays a more subdued crowd calls by for a night of Scandinavian electronic music. Bottled Becks is the beer of choice, which revellers spill and swill

well into the night. It is not exactly the place to debut a pair of Manolo Blahnik's – practical clothing should be chosen accordingly. Swap the designer threads for thrift-shop finds, and there shouldn't be a problem.

Maria Am Ostbahnhof, An der Schillingbrücke, Friedrichshain
Tel: 2123 8190 www.clubmaria.de
Open: 11pm–open-end Fri, Sat

Industrial minimalism doesn't get much better than at this waterside warehouse underneath the Schillingbrücke. The super-size sound system makes it a great location for live events and daring club nights. As is typical of clubs in Berlin, the music policy depends largely on the party being held – but the playlist in Maria is generally electronic and progressive. The Transmediale festival also takes place here every year. When filled to capacity, Maria is the best warehouse rave in town; when empty, it's just a cold open space. During summer, the grassy riverbanks are littered with bodies and beer cans. The crowd is mixed, but only those willing to put up with surface dirt and grime can survive.

Come here when the queues for nearby Berghain are too long to consider.

**Pavillon, Friedenstraße im Volkspark,
Platz de Vereinten Nationen, Friedrichshain**
Tel: 750 4724 www.pavillon-berlin.de
Open: 11pm–open-end Fri, Sat; beer garden from 11am in summer

Once a famous GDR restaurant, this park pavilion now hosts regular club events. Particularly popular are the Soul Explosion nights, which take place on the second and the last Saturdays of the month. Guests arrive in full '70s garb to strut their stuff underneath a sparkling glitter ball. One of the best funk parties in town, it always attracts a fun crowd. The Pavillon also plays host to Berlin's Kerrera club, who regularly put on rock and

indie events around the city. Inside, comfy black leather sofas are perfect for reclining with a cocktail, while a large beer garden is open for lounging in the summer. The circular dance-floor has a school-disco vibe and the sound equipment is a little on the basic side, but a friendly atmosphere more than compensates. The Pavillon can be found near the edge of the Volkspark.

Polar.tv, Heidestraße 73, Mitte
Tel: 246 259 320 www.polartv.de
Open: 11pm–open-end Sat

Home to Berlin party squad No UFOs (borrowed from a record by Detroit DJ Juan Atkins), the music policy at Polar.tv is essentially techno and tech-house. Prior to finding their by-no-means-humble abode, the team would put on events three to four times a year at different locations around the city. These days the parties still attract an underground following, but are more regular and better publicized. The club lies on the periphery of Mitte in an area otherwise characterized by industrial train-tracks. The warehouse space comprises one main room and a smaller bar filled with sofas and TV screens. The look is industrial and almost space age. In the summer, an outdoor area (complete with rock pool and sand pit) provides ample entertainment for those seeking a breath of fresh air. Expect to catch international favourites such as Laurent Garnier and Etienne d'Crecy.

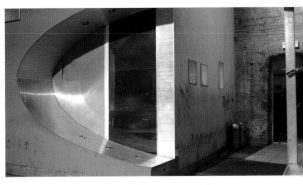

Sage, Köpenicker Straße 76, Mitte
Tel: 278 9830 www.sage-club.de
Open: from 7pm Wed; 10pm Thurs; 11pm Fri, Sat; 6am Sun

Berlin's answer to the Ministry of Sound, Sage is a super club of epic proportions. Fitting every stereotype going, Sage does exactly what it says on the packet. It's easy to lose yourself in the labyrinthine rooms, where different DJs spin an eclectic mix of styles, making a sharp exit virtually impossible. Fire-breathing dragons and fake water features are met with approval from its affluent and glamorous crowd. Mainstream house and techno are served up regularly, making Sage a good common denominator for an undecided crowd. An after-hours party takes place on Sundays, cutting well into your day of rest. Dress to impress.

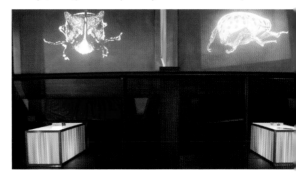

Stern Radio, Alexanderplatz 5, Mitte
Tel: 246 259 320 www.sternradio-berlin.de
Open: 11pm (10pm Tues)–open-end Fri, Sat; 8am–6pm Sun

Also home to the No UFOs party team (see Polar.tv), this smaller club attracts an inner-city crowd. Focusing mainly on house music, the club is consistently busy and attracts a young crowd of cool kids in jeans and trainers. Tucked behind the office block Haus des Reisens, Stern Radio was once a GDR restaurant. There's no stringent dress code, but the crowd leans towards the more musically discerning and dress to suit their choice of scene. On Tuesday nights, the venue hosts a very different soul/hip-hop event in conjunction with hip-hop party organizers Live Demo. And if the weekend doesn't start in Stern Radio, it certainly ends here: popular after-hours party 'Blaue Stunde' kicks off here at 8am every Sunday morning.

Watergate, Falckensteinstraße 49, Kreuzberg
Tel: 6128 0395 www.water-gate.de
Open: 11pm–open-end Thurs–Sat.

Easily the most accessible of Berlin's cool club clique, this sleek-looking venue runs itself along the lines of London's Fabric. Boasting one of the better sound systems in Berlin, it's a great place to catch both live bands and top-name DJs. Nestled just below the Oberbaumbrücke, a lower-level dance-floor looks directly onto the River Spree. Through the giant glass windows it's possible to watch the odd boat floating past and, in winter, the odd block of ice. During summer months, an outdoor deck caters for spaced-out star-gazers and sophisticated moon-bathers. As daylight breaks, many revellers sneak upstairs to the safe anonymity of a darker dance-floor. The clientele largely depends on the type of party thrown (from record release parties to electro tech-fests), but expect to find a crowd of style-savvy tastemakers. Of all the clubs in Berlin, Watergate is easily the cleanest, possibly the most comfortable – but definitely the most clinical. Tip: head for the forgotten upstairs bar near the ladies' lavatories for faster service. And girls, while you're here,

check out the loo with a view to the river.

Those who give up easily shouldn't even bother with Weekend, which is painfully trendy (even by Berlin standards). But if tapping into the Berlin party scene flicks your switch and you're truly up for a challenge – this could be your best match yet. In time-honoured tradition, demand creates demand and by virtue of being 'underground' this is the party everyone wants to attend. Arrive with a big group of blokes and you probably won't get in, but latch on to either a cool-cut local or a pretty girl and you should just about make the grade. The entrance itself isn't quite so assuming – just the revolving doors to a white-collar worker

office block. Once inside, take the lift to the 15th floor where the party is in full swing. The music policy is mainly trendy tech house and electro; organizers F.U.N. are well known and respected on the party circuit. If the outfits on parade aren't tantalizing enough, fantastic views of the Alex tower will certainly keep you occupied. Worth a visit to see what all the fuss is about.

WMF, Stralauer Straße 58, Mitte
Tel: 2804 2165   www.wmfclub.de
Open: 11pm–open-end Sat (and occasional Fridays)

The WMF have survived several incarnations and made the transformation from ad-hoc rave to regular club night whilst successfully retaining their cool. Having played at the famous Café Moskau and the Palais de la République (once the heart of East Berlin), the collective have now settled at an old office block on Stralauer Straße. Lit only be eerie red and green lights, the long corridors split off into several small rooms filled with a TV screens, decks and (oddly) a double divan. The main dance-floor boasts a slick sound system, perfect for the many live bands and techno DJs who play. Music varies according to the party, but eclectically ranges from techno and electronic to hip-hop and grime. The WMF also host the legendary Beep Street parties and

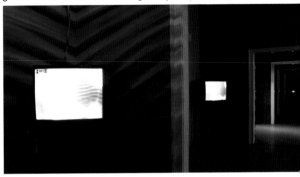

their main events are well publicized, but it's still worth checking in advance. Attracting a cool cosmopolitan crowd, this is one of the best parties in town.

Yaam @ Hoppetosse, Eichenstraße 4, Treptow
Tel: 5332 0340 www.arena-berlin.de
Open: 10pm–open-end Sun

Berlin's premier reggae party takes place every Sunday night on
the moored Hoppetosse boat. Rastas, students and music lovers
dance well into the night, irrespective of whether or not they
have to make it to work in the morning. The air is often thick
with cannabis smoke and women should expect some friendly
attention on the dance-floor. But the mood is always upbeat, and
interesting characters a dead cert. Those desperate for a breath
of non-smoky air should head to the open deck up top. During
the week the boat also functions as a restaurant and hosts various electronic, rock and gay parties, but check the web for
details first. The boat dates back to the '30s and was used as a
hospital during the War. In 2000 it was dismantled and transport-
ed to Berlin. In the winter, Yaam also holds parties at Ostbahnhof
on Sundays from 2pm.

LIVE MUSIC

A-Trane, Bleibtreustraße 1, Charlottenburg
Tel: 313 2550 www.a-trane.de
Concerts from 10pm daily

This New York style jazz bar is always packed. Crowds clamber
for one of the small stage-side tables and performances are
always intimate. Expect top-class jazz, with free entry on
Mondays and Tuesdays.

Quasimodo, Kantstraße 12a, Charlottenburg
Tel: 312 8086 www.quasimodo.de
Concerts from 9pm daily

This is Berlin's oldest jazz club. The space is small, smoky and
claustrophobic, but the artists playing are always top-notch.
Expect to see faces every scene: traditional, modern, blues, roots
and R&B. An airy café upstairs provides light relief.

Unique, Kantstraße 17, Charlottenburg
Tel: 315 1860 www.unique-music-lounge.de
Concerts from 8.30pm Mon–Thurs; 10pm Fri–Sun

Enjoy trad-jazz dining on a large scale at this popular venue. Part of the Stilwerk building, the interior was designed by Terence Conran. Expect to see top names in a smart setting, but be aware that it lacks the intimacy and atmosphere of smaller jazz clubs.

ADULT ENTERTAINMENT

Ever since the 1920s, Berlin has enjoyed an open-minded approach to sex. Cabaret has long been a Berlin tradition and a socially acceptable form of sexual entertainment. The city's main red-light district can be found along the Oranienburgerstraße, where eastern European girls cruise for clients. Bizarrely, they all tend to dress identically and even opt for bustiers over their bomber jackets during particularly cold winters. Although discreet, there are several clues to indicate a city brothel – mainly a woman's forename above a buzzer. Berlin also caters for fetish fanatics; the infamous KitKatClub is the most accessible of all the clubs.

KitKatClub, Bessemerstraße 4, Schöneberg
Tel: none www.kitkatclub.de
Open: 9pm–late Thurs; 11pm–late Fri/Sat; 8pm–late Sun

Despite its reputation, the KitKat is not at all seedy. Admittedly every sexual activity under the sun takes place in dark nooks and crannies, but a sense of irresistible liberation hangs in the air. This den of decadence consists of a downstairs dance-floor and penthouse above. Entry is open to all, but you'll need to pass a strict erotic dress code. Basically, dress to undress or you probably won't get in. The Sunday morning Piep Show is always popular.

culture...

Much of Berlin's difficult and tumultuous history is reflected in the cityscape. Reminders of life under the Third Reich abound, although some of the most painful memories have been translated into more positive messages with investment made in projects such as Daniel Libeskind's Jüdisches Museum – a piece of architectural genius. The Bauhaus Archiv, a further point of architectural interest, gives a detailed history of the movement that came to shape city building and design from 1919 to 1933.

Five of Berlin's major museums, the Bode Museum, Pergamon Museum, Alte Nationalgalerie, Neues Museum and Altes Museum, are located on the Museuminsel ('museum island') at the eastern end of Unter den Linden. Because of its cultural importance, the Museuminsel was added to UNESCO's World Cultural Heritage list in 1999.

Berlin's more recent cultural history is documented in the eastern side of the city. The crumbling Tacheles building, once a shopping arcade, became a focus for free-party activity in the heady days following Reunification and is a fine example of squat living. A remaining section of the Berlin Wall stretches along Mühlenstraße in Friedrichshain. International artists were invited to decorate

sections and today it exists as a poignant work of art. Now considered a symbol of modern Berlin, the Fernsehturm (the Swedish-engineered TV tower) in Alexanderplatz has arguably become the city's most recognizable landmark.

Artists and creative types have long been attracted to the city and a strong art scene continues to flourish. The converted Hamburger Bahnhof presents some striking collections of modern art while the Sammlung Hoffman is an excellent example of a private gallery.

A strong theatre tradition also exists with an emphasis on experimental productions. The Schaubühne, Gorki Theatre, Berliner Ensemble and Volksbühne are key venues. The city also has six orchestras and three opera houses. The Berlin Philharmonic is considered to be one of the finest symphony orchestras in the world.

Synonymous with Berlin's Roaring '20s, cabaret continues to draw a crowd. The *Variete* shows at the Wintergarten and Pomp, Duck and Circumstance are expensive and feature mainly clowns, magicians and acrobats. A more authentic cabaret experience can be found at the Kleine Nachtrevue, while Bar Jeder Vernunft presents a modern interpretation (often with improvised-theatre and stand-up comedy) in the setting of a circus tent.

**Bauhaus Archiv – Museum für Gestaltung,
Klingelhöferstraße 13–14, Tiergarten**
Tel: 254 0020 www.bauhaus.de
Open: 10am–5pm. Closed Tuesdays.

The Berlin-based Bauhaus school (1919–33) had a massive influence on modern design. Famous members included Klee, Kandinsky and Schlemmer among others. A comprehensive history of the school can be found in this architecturally striking

building, opened in 1979. Designed by founder Walter Gropius, it looks a little like the smokestacks on an ocean liner. The collection includes furniture, ceramics, prints, sculptures, photographs and sketches created in the workshop before it was shut down by the Nazis. Look out for Laszlo Moholy-Nagy's kinetic sculpture combining colour, light and movement.

Berliner Fernsehturm, Panoramastraße 1A, Mitte.
Tel: 242 3333 www.berlinerfernsehturm.de
Open: Mar–Oct 9am–1am daily; Nov–Feb 10am–midnight daily

While our own telecommunications tower is remembered for hosting the Noel Edmonds' Christmas show, Berlin's TV tower has become an international landmark. In bad weather the red and white mast disappears almost completely in the fog, but on clear days it's a permanent fixture of the city's skyline. Built by Walter Ulbricht in Communist times, the 368-metre tower (also visible in the west) was intended as an assertion of power and dynamism. Taking four years to build, it was finally completed in 1969. Bizarrely, legend has it that when the sun shines on the tower, reflections on the ball form a cross – dubbed 'the Pope's

revenge'. Visitors can take a lift up to the observation tower – a great way to see the entire city in one short trip. A revolving restaurant serves food and snacks, but there is always a wait for tables.

East Side Gallery, Mühlenstraße, Friedrichshain

When the Berlin Wall fell in 1989, it marked the most dramatic event in Berlin's modern history. While much of it was destroyed or snapped up by entrepreneurial souvenir shops, a large stretch remains intact on the eastern bank of the Spree from

Ostbahnhof to the Oberbaumbrücke. The largest open-air gallery in the world (at 1,316 metres), it has now been marked as a listed building. After the Wall fell, 118 artists from 21 countries were invited to paint murals. Especially famous is *The Mortal Kiss* by Dimitrij Vrubel, showing Erich Honecker and Leonid Brezhnev kissing. Although inspired by worthy intentions, much of the work is far less impressive than the street art and graffiti for which Berlin is world-famous.

Hamburger Bahnhof, Invaladienstraße 50–51, Mitte
Tel: 397 8340 www.smpk.de
Open: 10am–6pm Tues–Fri; 11am–6pm Sat, Sun

The striking façade of this former railway station is an indication of its newer incarnation as a museum of ultra-modern and conceptual art. Dan Flavin's stunning blue and green fluorescent light installation is particularly impressive after dark. The permanent collection was bequeathed mainly by Erich Marx and includes

wings by Andy Warhol (with some great pre-Pop Art drawings from the 1950s) and Joseph Beuys (with a video archive of all his taped performances). Other pieces can be found by Sol LeWitt, Bruce Nauman, Anselm Kiefer and many others. Temporary exhibitions from a range of prominent contemporary artists can be found on the upper floors. The café is pleasant, and the bookshop fantastic.

Jüdisches Museum, Lindenstraße 9–14, Kreuzberg
Tel: 2599 3300 www.jmberlin.de
Open: 10am–8pm (10pm Mon) daily

Rather a celebration and assertion of Jewish history than a gory
detailing of the Holocaust, Daniel Libeskind's creation is one of
the most thought-provoking structures of our modern times. (He
is also responsible for the World Trade Centre memorial plans.)
Designed as a compressed and distorted six-point star, the zig-zag
zinc-clad building is divided into three major areas. The Holocaust

tower is a long, concrete, cold tower, with just one slit of light.
This leads to the Garden of Exile, the only completely square
form in the building, comprising 48 densely compacted concrete
columns. These are filled with Berlin soil and represent the for-
mation of a Jewish state in 1948. A single central column is filled
with sand from Jerusalem and stands for Berlin itself. The
Memory Void is a place for contemplation, with a striking installation by Israeli artists Menashe Kadishman. The museum incorporates a far more detailed history of Jewish–German life.

Pergamonmuseum, Am Kupfergraben, Mitte
Tel: 2090 5566 www.smpk.de
Open: 10am–6pm (10pm Thurs). Closed Mondays.

The Pergamon is one of the world's finest archeological museums and includes collections of Classical and Near-Eastern

175

antiquities. The museum takes its name from the 16-metre high Pergamon Altar of Zeus that dates back to a 164 BC royal temple in Bergama, Turkey; a partial recreation can be found inside with an original frieze, depicting a battle between the gods and

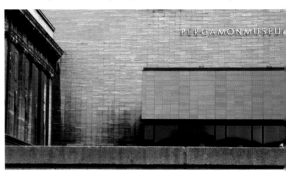

the titans, that once wound 113 metres around the base. The grand Roman Market Gate of Miletus (AD 120) and the tiled Gate of Ishtar form the other major attractions. Despite the number of works exhibited, the museum is easily digestible, but if you're craving more, the Museum of Islamic Art can be found in the southern wing. The Pergamon is part of the Museuminsel – an island in the Spree donated to 'art and science' by Friedrich Wilhelm IV and home to four other major museums. All are overlooked by Berlin's Protestant cathedral, the Berliner Dom. Take a trip to the upper balcony for stunning views of the island.

Reichstag, Platz der Republik 1, Mitte
Tel: 2273 2152 www.bundestag.de
Open: 8am–12am daily (last admission 10pm)

At one time wrapped in fabric by Bulgarian artist Christo, the German Parliamentary building has never been shy of controversy. Originally built by Paul Wallot in 1894, it suffered an arson attack in 1933 which was used by the Nazis as a pretext to clamp down on Communists. Sir Norman Foster was responsible for the impressive renovations in 1999 – a blend of old and new. Original graffiti from Russian soldiers in 1945 remains on the walls and can make for interesting reading. Queues can be long, but a trip to the top of the Reichstag's glass dome is a must. If the city views aren't impressive enough, the mirror-clad funnel at the centre of the dome (used to shed light on workers below) will visually amuse. The highly regarded Dachgarten restaurant can also be found beneath the dome. Note: access to the Reichstag interior and Plenary Hall is by prior arrangement only.

Schloß Charlottenburg, Spandauer Damm 20–24
Tel: 3209 1440 www.spsg.de
Open: 9am (10am Sat/Sun)–6pm. Closed Monday.

Built in 1695 as a summer residence for Friedrich I and Queen Sophia-Charlotte, this is the largest surviving Hohenzollern Palace. The huge gardens are a particular draw, with a Belvedere teahouse built in 1788. The Palace itself is vast and various combination entrance tickets can be purchased: save yourself a headache and go for the combined ticket. Much of the Old Palace is classically traditional, dripping with silver and porcelain. Of more interest is the New Wing of the state apartments of Frederick the Great. A collector of 18th-century French art, he accumulated many impressive works. The Stüler Bau Pavilion can also be found in the castle grounds and houses the Sammlung Berggruen, with a collection of works by Picasso, Cézanne, Van Gogh and Klee.

Sammlung Hoffman, Sophienstraße 21, Mitte
Tel: 2849 9121 www.sophie-gips.de
Open: 11am–4pm Sat (by appointment only)

There are plenty of hidden surprises awaiting discovery behind
Berlin's many courtyards. Gunda Förster's neon-light installation
bathes this particular courtyard in lurid yellows, blues and reds.
Once a sewing-machine factory and manufacturer of medical
equipment, the complex is now home to the Sammlung Hoffman
– a private collection of contemporary art. Owners Erika and
Rolf Hoffman have been collecting art for 30 years and open
their house to the public by appointment (felt slippers are provided). Actual displays change every year, but the floor installation
by Swiss video artist Pipilotti Rist is well worth checking out.

Tacheles, Oranienburger Straße 54–56, Mitte
Tel: 282 6185 www.tacheles.de

Even in its derelict and crumbling state, there's something truly
captivating about this 1908 shopping arcade – perhaps because it
is such a poignant reminder of our none-too-distant past. Used
by various Nazi organizations, it was bombed during the War
and hasn't been repaired since. The GDR tried to demolish it,
but ran out of dynamite halfway through. During the '90s, in the
post-Reunification squatters' heyday, a group of artists and party
organizers moved in with families in tow. It's now one of the last
remaining squats in Mitte and a memory of post-Wall Berlin. In
1998 a German company moved in to buy Tacheles and recon-
structed a large part of the building. Working artists' studios are

open to the public and film showings also take place in the cinema downstairs.

BALLET, OPERA AND CONCERTS

Deutsche Oper, Bismarckstraße 35, Charlottenburg
Tel: 343 8401 www.detscheoperberlin.de
Box office: 11am–30mins before performance Mon–Fri;
10am–2pm Sat

Berlin's largest opera house dates back to 1912 and the current
concert hall was built in 1961. Since Reunification, however, it has

been overshadowed by the more aesthetically pleasing Staatstoper. Regardless, a reputation for classic productions remains untouched. The house specialty is Wagner and Oper principle conductor Christian Thielemann is an expert in his field. More recently, contemporary works have been introduced, including masterpieces from 20th-century composers such as Bartok. All performances are given in their original language. Unsold tickets are available at a discount price before shows.

Philharmonie, Herbert-von-Karajan Straße 1, Tiergarten
Tel: 2548 8999 www.berlin-philharmonic.com
Box office: 9am–6pm daily

This striking piece of modern architecture is easily the most famous concert hall in Berlin and home to the world-renowned Berlin Philharmonic Orchestra. The shimmering golden structure was designed by Hans Scharoun and opened in 1963. The acoustics are incredible in front of the orchestra, where seats are accordingly the most expensive. Elsewhere they can vary. The Orchestra was founded in 1882 and has been led by some of the world's finest conductors; it's currently in the hands of innovator Sir Simon Rattle. Aside from more traditional compositions, he has introduced work from contemporary composers and collaborations with jazz artists and improvisers. About 100 performances are given throughout the year (except July) and a few tickets are often available directly before each show. Tickets can otherwise be difficult to secure and should be booked up to eight weeks in advance. The building also has a smaller hall, the Kammermusiksaal.

Staatsoper Unter den Linden, Unter den Linden 5-7, Mitte
Tel: 203 540/tickets 2035 4555 www.staatsoper-berlin.de
Box office: 10am–8pm Mon–Sat, 2–8pm Sun

Founded as Prussia's Royal Court Opera for Frederick the Great in 1742, the Staatsoper suffered immense damage in World War II. The current building dates from 1955, although great effort has been taken to replicate the original elegant design. Sadly, it's still in desperate need of renovation. It's orchestra, the Berliner Staatskapelle, is considered to be Berlin's finest opera orchestra and is under the direction of Daniel Barenboim, while 'Dancer of the century' Vladimir Malakhov has been ballet director since 2002. The programme runs traditional ballet and opera performances with chamber music performed in the Apollo Saal, along with the occasional electronic music event. Unsold tickets are available for €10 before the start of each show.

THEATRE

Berliner Ensemble, Bertolt-Brecht-Platz 1, Mitte
Tel: 2840 8155   www.berliner-ensemble.de
Box Office: 8am–6pm Mon–Fri; 11am–6pm Sat–Sun

This theatre was made famous by its association with the father of German theatre, Bertolt Brecht. He ran the place from 1948 until his death in 1956, with his *Threepenny Opera* staged here in 1928. Actor and director Max Reinhardt also produced plays for the Berliner Ensemble. Today, Viennese director Claus Peymann is at the helm and you can expect modern productions from Austrian and German writers alongside Brecht and Shakespeare. The building itself is stunning.

Maxim Gorki Theatre, Am Festungsgraben 2, Mitte
Box office: 2022 1115, Info 2022 1129   www.gorki.de
Box office: midday (4pm Sun)–6.30pm daily

This small theatre presents a mixture of traditional and contemporary productions and has a good reputation for progressive Russian and Eastern European drama. Plays are usually funny, thoughtful and innovative. It's a good place to catch next generation talent, and actor and director Katharina Thalbach always draws a crowd. Chekhov is a firm favourite here.

Schaubühne am Lehniner Platz, Kurfürstendamm 153, Charlottenburg
Tel: 890 023 www.schabühne.de
Box office: 11am (3pm Sun)–6.30pm daily

This former 1920s cinema and Bauhaus construction is now a highlight on Berlin's cutting-edge theatre scene. The programme features contemporary dance and drama productions from young international authors. English-language works are also presented. At the helm are internationally acclaimed choreographer Sasha Waltz and director Thomas Ostermeier. After-show drinks can be taken in the fashionable theatre cocktail bar, the Universum Lounge.

Volksbühne, Rosa-Luxemburg Platz, Mitte
Tel: 247 6772 www.volksbühne-berlin.de

This 'People's Stage' follows a radical, non-conformist form and is never afraid of controversy. This is largely thanks to maverick Frank Castorf and his team of provocative guest directors. The theatre accordingly attracts a young and fashionable East Berlin crowd. The imposing building dates back to 1913 and was built by Oskar Kaufmann. Two salons also run independent events: the Roter (red) Salon often runs electronic club nights and after-show parties for music concerts held in the Volksbühne; the Grüner (green) Salon is the preserve of a more sedate crowd and holds a weekly salsa night every Thursday. Smaller performances also take place at the Volksbühne am Prater, Kastanianallee 7–9.

CABARET

Bar Jeder Vernunft, Spiegelzelt, Schaperstraße 24, Wilmersdorf
Tel: 883 1582 www.bar-jeder-vernunft.de
Box office: midday–7pm daily

A former circus tent provides the unique setting for this modern cabaret company. Founded by Holger Klotzbach in 1992, shows are a mixture of musical, political satire and comedy. Red velvet, brass and mirrors make for an opulent but intimate interior and food is provided by restaurant Florian. Drinks can be pricey. Tickets cost €15–30.

Kleine Nachtrevue, Kufürstenstraße 116, Schöneberg
Tel: 218 8950 www.kleine-nachtrevue.de
Open: 7pm–3am. Closed Sunday and Monday.

The most authentic cabaret experience you'll find in Berlin. Shows are risqué, although nudity is always tasteful. Special shows take place at 9pm on weekends and are usually of an erotic flavour. Shows cost €15–25.

Pomp, Duck and Circumstance, Spiegelpalast Salon Zazou, Gleisdreieck/Möckernstraße 26, Kreuzberg
Tel: 2694 9200 www.pompduck.de
Box office: 9am–8pm Mon–Fri; midday–8pm Sat/Sun.

Extravagant shows are performed in this old-fashioned tent and are always reliably entertaining. A four-course meal is served (usually including duck), although tables are usually booked very quickly. Prices are high (€110–120) and the food sometimes under par.

Wintergarten Variete, Potsdammer Straße 96, Tiergarten
Tel: 2500 8888 www.wintergarten-variete.de
Box office: 10am–4pm. Closed Sunday.

This large, ostentatious venue puts on lavish shows every night with top magicians, clowns and acrobats. Shows are professionally choreographed, but can be of a mixed quality and change three or four times every year. Show and dinner tickets cost €66–76.

shop...

Essentially a fractured city, Berlin has no distinctive shopping centre. Instead retailers have sprouted up all over, although those of a similar type prefer to congregate around each other.

There are two main shopping drags: Friedrichstraße in the East and the almighty Kurfürstendamm (Ku'damm) in the West. Here you'll find all the international big brand designer names and the city's main shopping centres. Dussmann Das KulturKaufhaus, Galeries Lafayette and Quartier 206 are the major department stores on Friedrichstraße. The KaDeWe, Berlin's answer to Harrods, is located at the Tauentzienstraße end of the Ku'damm, and smaller designer boutiques can be found in the streets between Ku'damm and Kantstraße. The Stilwerk on Kantstraße is a one-stop destination for style-savvy home-improvers.

Although in a different league from Paris and New York, Berlin is still a leading light in the realm of young, independent fashion design. Some styles are outlandish, while others follow street fashion. In Mitte, most boutiques line the streets of Alte and Neue Schönhauser and Hackesche Höfe. The Kastanianallee in Prenzlauer Berg is a good source of cutting-edge design. There are also numerous comic-book and graphic-design stores in Mitte, presumably a reflec-

tion of the high concentration of media businesses in this area. Commercial art galleries can be found along Auguststraße.

Other areas worthy of mention are the Simon-Dach Straße in Friedrichshain (good for young, affordable fashions) and the Bergmannstraße in Kreuzberg (homeware and more conservative styles).

Berlin has many antique dealers and bric-à-brac shops, making it a treasure-hunter's paradise. The area around Goltzstraße in Schöneberg is good for 18th- and 19th-century finds, while Fasanenplatz in Wilmersdorf is also worth a visit. The KPM brand of porcelain is world-famous, and can be purchased from their shop in Tiergarten. Retro pieces of GDR styling are also considered a nostalgic souvenir. Chunks of the wall can still

be purchased and design stores such as Eastberlin have incorporated iconography from the East (such at the Fernsehturm and the very unique traffic-light men) into their fashion designs.

Berlin is famous for its markets – most notably the Christmas markets, which take place in the city throughout December. The well-stocked flea markets also offer up a bargain or two – from vintage clothing, retro furnishings and old audio equipment to house clearance curios and antique jewellery. One man's junk is another man's treasure and you'll have to dig deep to reap rewards. As you'll quickly come to expect in Berlin, there's no point in turning up early – most stallholders won't even be out of bed when the markets open.

Other good markets worth checking are the farmers' market on Wittenbergplatz (Tues–Fri), the Türkischer Markt at Maybachufer (Tues and Fri), the Kollwitzplatz market (Thurs and Sat) and the Winterfeldmarkt on Winterfeldplatz (Wed and Sat).

BOOKS

Kochlust, Alte Schönhauser Straße 36–37, Mitte – cookbook shop (most titles in English) with demonstration kitchen out the back

Pro QM, Alte Schönhauser Straße 48, Mitte – a former butcher's shop selling architectural and design books

DEPARTMENT STORES

Galeries Lafayette, Französische Straße 23, Mitte – a Berlin branch of the famous Parisian department store

KaDeWe, Tauentzienstrasse 21–24, Charlottenburg – a place of consumer worship. The ultimate design superstore on a par with Harrods and Harvey Nicks.

Quartier 206, Friedrichstraße 71, Mitte – upmarket department store with designer clothes, cosmetics and homeware

DESIGN/ART

Bless, Mulackstraße 38, Mitte – avant-garde design store selling clothes, artworks, shoes and accessories

Blindenanstalt Berlin, Oranienstraße 26, Kreuzberg – imaginative souvenirs and obscure design items

Deco Arts, Motzstraße 6, Schöneberg – art-deco furniture and antique treasures from the '50s and '60s

Dopo Domani, Kantstraße 148, Charlottenburg – Italian design products in a townhouse setting

Kramari, Gneisenaustraße 91, Kreuzberg – furniture and home accessories from the Bauhaus to the '70s

Nix, Oranienburger Straße 32, Mitte – comfortable, simple textiles from Barbara Gebhardt

Radio Art, Zossener Straße 2, Kreuzberg – antique radios from the '30s to the '70s, all in perfect working order

Re-Store, Auguststraße 3, Mitte – designers Vaike Fuchs and Stefan Wecker transform industrial waste into desirable products

Room Safari, Sweinemünder Straße 6, Prenzlauer Berg – innovative product design for everyday living

Schmidt Antik, Detmolder Straße 59, Wilmersdorf – antique dealers. A journey through 20th-century kitsch, design and artwork.

Stilwerk, Kantstraße 17, Charlottenburg – furniture and design complex with products from 500 brands

Supalife Kiosk, Raumerstraße 40, Prenzlauer Berg – Showcase space for local talent. Sells original artwork and street clothing.

FASHION

Adidas Originals Store, Munzstraße 13–15, Mitte – flagship design store for the 'three-stripe' institution

Andreas Murkudis, Munzstraße 21, Mitte – clothes and accessories from next-generation designers

Antonie Setzer, Bleibtreustraße 19, Charlottenburg – designer womenswear from D&G, Miu Miu and many others

Apartment, Memhardtstraße 8, Mitte – exclusive store hidden in a courtyard, stocking young international design for women and men

A.P.C., Mulackstraße 35, Mitte – womenswear and menswear from Jean Touitou in a new flagship store from the French cult brand

Betty Bund Store, Rosa-Luxembourg Straße 15, Mitte – colourful, fun and outrageous clothing from local designers

Carhartt Store, Rosenthaler Straße 48, Mitte – street fashion from the German brand

Chiton, Goltzstraße 12, Schöneberg – designer bridal and evening gowns from Robert and Friederike Jorzig

Claudia Skoda, Alte Schönhauser Straße 35, Mitte – knitwear from legendary designer, who started out in 1970s Kreuzberg and dressed the likes of David Bowie and Tina Turner

Crème Fresh, Kastanianallee 21, Prenzlauer Berg – trend pieces from young designers all over Europe

Eastberlin, Alte Schönhauser Straße 33–34, Mitte – patriotic shop with trend designs incorporating key elements of the city. Street fashion.

Fiebelkorn and Kuckuck, Bleibtreustraße 4, Charlottenburg – bridal wear and evening dress from two conflicting designers sharing the same space

GB, Auguststraße 77/78, Mitte – classic cult clothing produced in two sizes or made to measure

Hasipop, Oderberger Straße 39, Prenzlauer Berg – pop trash fashions from several young aspiring designers

Herz & Stöhr, Winterfeldstraße 52, Schöneberg – innovative and feminine designs from well-respected design duo

Holly, Alte Schönhauser Straße 4, Mitte – designer streetwear in a '50s-styled interior – boudoir lounge, housing the work of 12 designers

Hut Up, Oranienburger Straße 32, Mitte – felt creations in bright colours from Christine Birkle

Jil Sander, Kurfürstendamm 185, Charlottenburg – carries her complete line of understated clothing

Killerbeast, Schlesische Straße 31, Kreuzberg – cool outfits made from recycled material with an eco-friendly range

Konk, Raumerstraße 36, Prenzlauer Berg – design trends that are both elegant and street

Lisa D, Rosenthaler Straße 40–41, Mitte – feminist activist designing women's clothes

Lucid 21, Mariannestraße 50, Kreuzberg – kitsch, contemporary and arty clothes and accessories from the Berlin-based fashion label

Mientus Studio 2002, Wilmersdorfer Straße 73, Charlottenburg – international and German designer menswear from labels including Helmut Lang and Miu Miu

Molotow, Gneisenaustraße 112, Kreuzberg – fashion and millinery from local talents

Mutablis, Stubbenkammerstraße 4, Prenzlauer Berg – three female designers, with lines in 'trend', 'young classics' and 'evening fashion'

Patrick Hellman, Fasanenstraße 29, Charlottenburg – tailor-made fashions for men and women using designer textiles

Sabine Kneiesche, Knaackstraße 33, Prenzlauer Berg – where fashion becomes art

Schelpmeier, Knaackstraße 20a, Prenzlauer Berg – modern, but classic fashions from Germany and Scandinavia

Schmuckgalerie Aquamarin, Bergmannstraße 20, Kreuzberg – designer-wear from Germany, Switzerland and Denmark

Starstyling, Rosenthaler Straße 50, Mitte – style store for fashion victims

T&G, Rosenthaler Straße 34–35, Mitte – bold and striking interior offering equally outrageous fashions from Alexander McQueen, Givenchy and Vivienne Westwood

Thatchers, Kastanianallee 21, Prenzlauer Berg – modern collections for women inspired by music, video, photography and architecture

To Die For, Neue Schönhauser Straße 10, Mitte – mid-range design from labels such as D&G

Van Ravenstein, Leibnitzstraße 49, Charlottenberg – exclusive fashions from Dries van Norten, Martin Margiela and Ann Demeulemeester

FASHION ACCESORIES

Bag Ground, Gipsstraße 23b, Mitte – hand-made bags in all colours and materials

Chapeaux, Bleibtreustraße 51, Charlottenburg – Andrea Curti creates functional hats with style and personality

Milkberlin, Almstadtstraße 5, Mitte – robust, waterproof and cult bags

Penthesileia, Tucholsystraße 31, Mitte – strong, feminine and shapely bags

Schuhtanten, Paul-Linke-Ufer 44, Kreuzberg – designer clothes, accessories and bags from Danish and German designers

TaschenDesign Accessories, Torstraße 97, Mitte – bag and accessory design in contrasting colours and animal prints from a young Berlin designer

Tausche, Raumerstraße 8, Prenzlauer Berg – design-friendly bags for all purposes

FLEA MARKETS

The flea markets of Berlin are a bargain-hunter's paradise! Most homes (and bars, for that matter) are decked out in retro furnishings and curious objects purchased from the markets listed below.

Am Mauerpark, Bernauer Straße, Prenzlauer Berg. 10am–6pm Sun.

Large and lively market favoured by a young crowd. Great café with music.

Arena, Schlesische Straße/Eichenstraße, Treptow. 10am–6pm Sat, Sun

Original '60s and '70s furniture for sale in an old factory hall.

Boxhagener Platz, Friedrichshain. 9am–4pm Sun

Small market, with great selection and stalls from several local artists.

Kunst und Nostalgie Markt, Museuminsel, Mitte. 11am–5pm Sat, Sun

A place to pick up some old GDR relics.

Marheinekeplatz, Kreuzberg. 10am–4pm Sat, Sun

Records, books and retro furnishings can be found at this small market.

Rathaus Schöneberg, John-F-Kennedy Platz, Schöneberg. 9am–4pm Sat, Sun
Market selling electronic equipment, knick-knacks, clothes and shoes.

Straße des 17. Juni, Tiergarten. 10am–5pm Sat, Sun
Long stretch selling antiques and curios. Can be touristy.

Zille-Hof, Fasanenstraße 14, Charlottenburg. 8am–5.30pm Mon–Fri; 8am–1pm Sat
Junk and bric-à-brac market.

FOOD AND WINE

Absinth-Depot Berlin, Weinmeisterstraße 4, Mitte – 20 varieties of absinthe from family-run manufacturers in Spain and France, along with their own 60% proof variety

Frischparadies Lindenberg, Morsestraße 2, Charlottenburg – gourmet food store

Hamann-Bittere Schokoladen, Brandenburgische Straße 17 – Classic Berlin institution, producing chocolate since 1928.

In't Veld Schokoladen, Dunkerstraße 10, Prenzlauer Berg – gourmet chocolate from all corners of the globe

Kaaswinkel, Berlinerstraße 36, Wilmersdorf – specialist cheese shop

Teesalon, Invaladienstraße 160, Mitte – fantastic selection of teas

Die Weinlieferanten, Mohrenstraße 30, Mitte – a mecca for wine enthusiasts

Zigarren Herzog, Ludwigkirchplatz 1, Charlottenburg – an A–Z

of cigar smoking with walk-in humidor

HOME AND LIFESTYLE

1001 & 1 Seife, Sophienstraße 28–29, Mitte – hand-made soaps in delicious flavours

Belladonna, Bergmannstraße 101, Kreuzberg – natural beauty products from Logona, Lavera, Dr Hauschka and Weleda

Breathe, Rochstraaße 17, Mitte – natural beauty brands in a delightful setting; custom-made perfumes

Bürgel-Haus, Friedrichstraße 154, Mitte – blue and cream pottery from the state of Thüringen

Cara Tonga, Dirkenstraße 51, Prenzlauer Berg – where horticulture becomes an art form – fantastic flower arrangements favoured by a design crowd

Glasklar, Knesebeckstraße 13–14, Charlottenburg – glass objects ranging from the cheap to antique

Humpert & Suden, Pariser Straße 21, Wilmersdorf – furniture and home accessories at this florist and lifestyle concept shop

KPM, Unter den Linden 35, Mitte – porcelain given a seal of approval by Friedrich II in 1763

Kunst_Schule, Hufelandstraße 13, Prenzlauer Berg – hand-made household goods. Several art courses and a café available

RSVP Papier, Mulackstraße 14, Mitte – fine papers and writing materials

Wohnzimmer, Paul-Linke-Ufer 44, Kreuzberg – designer home accessories

Wolfgang Haus, Suarezstraße 3, Charlottenburg – period furniture from the last two centuries, with a good crystal selection

JEWELLERY

Fritz, Dresdener Straße 20, Kreuzberg – bold, hand-crafted jewellery for extremely special occasions
Glanzstücke, Sophienstraße 7, Mitte – Art Nouveau and Art Deco costume jewellery
Rio, Bleibtreustraße 52, Charlottenburg – vibrant jewellery based around vintage stones, acrylic beads and metalwork

Tosh, Sredzkistraße 56, Prenzlauer Berg – striking and artistic jewellery from celebrity favourite Thomas Schwender

LINGERIE

Blush, Rosa-Luxembourg Straße 22–24, Mitte – high-class underwear store
Les Dessous, Fasanenstraße 42, Wilmersdorf – luxury lingerie and swimwear
Fishbelly, Sophienstraße 7a, Mitte – imaginative designer lingerie; Berlin's answer to Agent Provocateur
Korsett Engelke, Kantstraße 109, Charlottenburg – hand-made corsets and bustiers for all sizes
Mane Lange Korsetts, Hagenauer Straße 13, Prenzlauer Berg – hand-made corsets from Mane Lange
Revanche de la Femme, Uhlandstraße 50, Charlottenburg – beautiful corsets in styles ranging from the traditional to avant-garde

MEN'S TAILORING

Harvey's, Kurfürstendamm 156, Charlottenberg – designer menswear from Japan and Belgium

Herr von Eden, Alte Schönhauser Straße 7, Mitte – modern, tailored suits inspired by '20s and '40s signs

Respectmen, Neue Schönhauser Straße 14, Mitte – classic cuts for men

Yoshiharu Ito, Auguststraße 19, Mitte – Japanese designer of menswear limited to six pieces per collection

MUSIC

Digalittledeeper, Torstraße 102, Mitte – predominantly hip-hop, soul and funk reissues

Freak Out, Rykestraße 23, Prenzlauer Berg – well-stocked electronic music store.

Vapo-Records, Danziger Straße 31, Prenzlauer Berg – cult record shop for punk and hardcore, with a small section for other styles

SHOES

Bleibgrun, Bleibtreustraße 29, Charlottenburg – Berlin's best designer shoe store

Fiona Bennett, Grosse Hamburger Straße 25, Mitte – elegant and extravagant footwear

Kirsten Henneman Masschuhmacherin, Sophienstraße 28–29, Mitte – tailor-made shoes for every need

Trainer, Alte Schönhauser Straße 50, Mitte – limited edition and rare trainers

Trippen, Knaackstraße 26, Prenzlauer Berg – wooden-soled and eco-friendly footwear

VINTAGE

Emma Emmelie, Schumanstraße 15a, Mitte – antique linens, vintage clothes and china dolls

Fingers, Nollendorfstraße 35, Schöneberg – eccentric knick-knacks from the '40s, '50s and '60s

play...

Like every cosmopolitan city, Berlin has a good range of facilities for both participating and spectator sports.

Although Germany has a good footballing reputation, the same is sadly not true of Berlin: Hertha Berlin seems to be more of a Charlton than a Chelsea these days. Germany will, however, play host to the 2006 World Cup with the final being played at Berlin's Olympiastadion. Originally built for the 1936 Olympics, it's an impressive example of Nazi monumentalist architecture.

Oddly, however, Berlin does excel in the field of beach volleyball. Approximately 3,000 tons of sand are deposited annually in Schlossplatz for the German Open, the most lucrative tournament on the German circuit. Although you'd be forgiven for thinking that Rio de Janeiro might make a more appropriate setting, Berlin is no less a contender in this traditionally seaside sport.

Continuing on a beach theme, there's ample opportunity to indulge in water sports – never has a land-locked city been so geared toward the aquatic. Sailing, motor-boating, canoeing and kayaking take place along the 200km net-

work of rivers, estuaries and canals. Windsurfing, waterskiing, wakeboarding and surfing are also popular pursuits. There are numerous swimming pools across the city, some in great historical locations (Stadtbad Charlottenburg and Stadtbad Mitte). A good outdoor pool for cooling off on hot summer days can be found at the Sommerbad Kreuzberg. There is even a pool built within the river, Badeschiff is a heated pool suspended in the river Spree, open during the summer the owners are considering turning it into a sauna and steam room in the winter. The cocktail bar makes it a truly decadent experience for a summer's afternoon.

Almost totally flat and well endowed with cycle lanes, Berlin is the perfect city to explore by bike. Many use it as a means of transport, but there are also plenty of scenic cycle routes to be enjoyed.

The notion of *Gesundheit* (health) is important to Berliners and many belong to local gyms. Unfortunately, most gyms require a minimum three-month contract, but the fitness centres listed here also offer a day rate. Many of the city's hotels are well-equipped with fitness facilities.

A rigorous workout is always best balanced with a relaxing spa or massage. 'Wellness' centres abound in the city, with several in every neighbourhood. The Liquidrom offers a unique experience: underwater sound speakers have been fitted in the thermal pool. Music events regularly take place, with all-nighters every full moon when guests can take a break from dancing to cool off with a massage.

BEACH VOLLEYBALL

It might seem an unlikely location, but Berlin is a premier spot for beach volleyball. The German Open is one of the biggest on the circuit, and Berlin played host to the World Championships in 2005.

City Beach am Friedrichshain, Kniprodestraße/Danziger Straße, Prenzlauerberg
Tel: 0177 247 6907 www.city-beach-berlin.de

There are nine courts at this outdoor facility (open all year round). Courts should be booked in advance. There's also a beach bar.

CANOEING

Kanu Connection, Köpenicker Straße 9, Kreuzberg
Tel: 612 2686 www.kanu-connection.de
Open: Mar–Oct: midday–7pm Tues–Fri; 9am–7pm Sat, Sun; Nov–Feb: 1pm–4pm Fri; 10am–4pm Sat

Berlin's extensive canal system is ideal for canoeing and kayaking. Hire boats for anything from three hours to a full day.

CYCLING

Flat, and well supplied with cycle lanes, Berlin is a haven for cyclists; there are few cities more suited to two-wheeled transportation. Bikes can be hired from Fahrradstation (tel: 2045 4500; www.fahrradstation.de).

ADFC Berlin, Brunnenstrasse 28, Mitte
Tel: 448 4724
Open: midday–8pm Mon–Fri; 10am–4pm Sat

This German bicycle club publishes a cycle route map of Berlin.

FOOTBALL

Hertha BSC, Olympischer Platz 3, Charlottenburg
Tel: 0180 518 9200 www.herthabsc.de

Berlin's local team has failed miserably to meet national expectations. Their ground, the Olympiastadion, is far more impressive. Built for the 1936 Olympics, it's one of the few examples of Nazi architecture that still remains intact. Kick-off is usually 3.30pm on Saturday. American football and athletics meets also take place here, along with the odd rock concert.

GOLF

**Golfpark Schloss Wilkendorf, Am Weiher 1,
OT Wilkendorf, Gielsdorf**
Tel: 03341 330 960 www.golfpark-schloss-wilkendorf.com
Open: Nov–Feb: 9am–5pm daily; Mar–Oct: 8am–7pm daily

This is the only 18-hole course in the area open to non-members. If you want to play at weekends, you'll need to have a Platzreife, a golf certificate obtainable by taking a test.

**Öffentliches Golf-Zentrum Berlin-Mitte,
Chauseestraße 94, Mitte**
Tel: 2804 7070 www.golfzentrum-berlin.de
Open: 7am–dusk daily

Housing a 64-tee driving range and roofed putting green, this facility is entirely free.

HORSE RACING

**Galopprennbahn Hoppegarten, Goetheallee 1,
Dahlwitz-Hoppegarten**
Tel: 03342 389 313/033 389 323
www.galopprennbahn-hoppegarten.de

Located in north-east Berlin, this 1867 race-course is one of the grandest in Europe. Thoroughbred races are held between April and October. All bets placed are shared among winners, along the lines of a British tote system.

Trabrennbahn Mariendorf, Mariendorfer Damm 222–298, Mariandorf
Tel: 740 1212 www.berlintrab.de

The Derby week, which takes place here in August, has become a major international event. Race meetings take place on Sundays at 1.30pm and Tuesdays at 6pm.

MOTOR-RACING

Eurospeedway Lausitz, Lausitzallee 1, Klettwitz
Tel: 035 754 31110/ 01805 880 288 www.eurospeedway.de

The German Touring Car Masters (DTM), the Porsche GTP weekend and International German Motorbike Championship (IDM) take place in Europe's largest racing facility. Novice racers can also take their own vehicles onto the track on certain days. The track lies 130km south-east of Berlin; take the A13 motor-way or the train to Senftenberg.

SPAS

ARS Vitalis, Hauptstraße 101, Schöneberg
Tel: 788 3563 www.ars-vitalis.de
Open: 8am–11.30pm daily

The combined gym and spa offers a good range of classes, three different types of sauna, a ladies-only area and massage. It's one of the best spots of this sort in Berlin and a day pass will set you back €25. A roof terrace can also be enjoyed in the summer.

Float Centre, Kronenstraße 55-58, Mitte
Tel: 2061 9933 www.floatcenter.de
Open: 10am–11pm daily

Enjoy complete relaxation in Berlin's first flotation tank centre. A one-hour session costs €50.

Hamam Turkish Bath, Schokoladenabrik, Mariannenstraße 6, Kreuzberg
Tel: 615 1464/615 2999 www.schokofabrik.de
Open: 3pm–11pm Mon; midday–10pm Tues–Sun

Women only can frequent this Turkish-style bathhouse. Guests are invited to enjoy tea, cake and fruit in a carpeted tearoom. The tiled hammam is lit from above with a heated platform in the centre. Massages can also be booked for 20-minute and 60-minute slots. A three-hour session costs €12.

Liquidrom, Möckernstraße 10
Tel: 7473 7171 www.liquidrom.com
Open: 10am–10pm Sun–Thurs; 10am–midnight Fri–Sat

The salt-water pool at the Liquidrom is unique: underwater speakers have been fitted by liquid-sound developer Micky Remann to make this a complete sensual experience. Music and light shows take place every weekend, with all-nighters every full moon. Massage and treatments are also available and cocktails can be ordered at the bar. A two-hour session costs €15.

Luxor Tempel of Wellness, Akazienstraße 28, Schöneberg
Tel: 7870 9507 www.luxor-berlin.com
Open: 11am–10pm. Closed Sundays.

Several different types of massage (from ayurvedic to full-body) are available in this Egyptian-styled centre, along with various beauty treatments. A number of packages are available. Ask for prices.

Surya Villa, Rykestraße 3, Prenzlauerberg
Tel: 4849 5780 www.ayurveda-wellnesszentrum.de
Open: 10.30am–9pm daily

Spread over four floors, this centre offers massage, baths, saunas, yoga, meditation and a holistic centre. A full day pass costs €165.

Thermen am Europa-Center, Nurnberger Strasse 7, Charlottenburg
Tel: 257 5760 www.thermen-berlin.de
Open: 10am–4am Mon–Sat; 10am–9pm Sun

Just off the Ku'damm, this stylish centre offers both indoor and outdoor thermal pools, nine saunas and several fitness rooms. A pleasant garden is open until October and a heated roof pool is available all year round. A day ticket costs €17.90.

SWIMMING

Contact the BBB for information on all Berlin's indoor, outdoor and lake-side swimming facilities. www.berlinerbaederbetriebe.de or tel: 01803102020.

Sommerbad Kreuzberg, Prinzenstrasse 113–119, Kreuzberg
Tel: 616 1080

Also known as the Prinzenbad ('Princes' Pool'), this is Berlin's most central open-air facility. There are two 50m pools (one for non-swimmers), a slide and a nudist area. Disabled access is also available. There's plenty of room for sunbathing, although on a hot day the place is heaving with teenagers.

Stadtbad Charlottenburg, Krumme Straße 10
Tel: Alte Halle 3438 3860; Neue Halle 3438 3865

The Art Nouveau ceiling and tiling of the Alte Halle date back to 1898 and the building is a protected monument. The 25m pool holds regular nude bathing nights, popular with gay men. The 50m Neue Halle is for more serious swimmers.

Stadtbad Mitte, Gartenstraße 5, Mitte
Tel: 3088 0910
Open: 6.30–10pm Mon, Wed; 10am–4pm Tues;
6.30am–8.30pm Thurs; 6.30am–10pm; 2–9pm Sat–Sun

The architecture of this unusual building alone is enough to draw the crowds. A renovated 1928 Bauhaus structure, a glass cube contains the 50m pool.

Strandbad Wannsee, Wanseebadweg 25, Zehlendorf
Tel: 803 5612 www.berlinerbaederbetriebe.de

Europe's largest lakeside pool boasts kilometres of sandy beach and decent water. It's been in operation since 1907 and is quite an institution. Visitors can rent boats, take exercise classes, hire pedalos or relax in the beer garden.

WATER SPORTS

Berlin is perfect for water sports. There are 50 lakes in the area and a 200m network of rivers, estuaries and canals. A licence is required for boating and sailing – a domestic one will suffice. Some contact details:

The Berlin-Brandenburg Water Sports Association (www.wtb-brb.de) has tourist maps of the waterways listing speed limits and landings.

The Wassersportzentrum Berlin (www.wassersportzen-trum.de) runs two centres with marinas in the Müggelsee (south-east Berlin).

If you're interested in waterskiing and wakeboarding, check out:

Wakeboard & Wasserski Grossbeeren (tel: 033701 90873 www.wassersport-grossbeeren.de) – a modern waterskiing facility.

Wet & Wild Wasserski-Seilbahn Berlin-Velten (tel: 0330 945 1563 www.wakeboard-berlin.de) – for boatless waterskiing.

AIRPORTS

There are currently three airports in Berlin: Tegel, Schönefeld and Temelhof.
Information in English on all of these can be found at www.berlin-airport.de

Tegel is 8km north-west of Mitte. The JetExpressBus TXL runs to
Alexanderplatz. A taxi to the middle of town will take about 30 minutes and
costs approximately €25. **Schönefeld** is the former airport of East Berlin and
18km south-east of the city. It's small, barren and mainly serviced by budget airlines. The S-bahn train station is a 5-minute walk from the airport; the Airport
Express runs to Alexanderplatz and the Zoo between 5am and 11.30pm and
takes 30 minutes. A taxi will cost approximately €35 and takes 50 minutes.
Templehof is the most central of the airports, 4km south of Mitte.
Unfortunately, few airlines fly here. The U-bahn station is a short walk from the
station and a taxi will take you to Mitte in 15 minutes for €12.

CLIMATE

Berlin is best visited during the summer months when temperatures are
around 25°C. Spring can be slow to arrive – usually in April. January and
February are the coldest months (-3°C) with winds blowing in from Siberia.
Skies can also be depressingly grey during the winter period – expect snow.

CYCLING

Completely flat and well equipped with cycle paths, Berlin is perfect for cycling
(see Play). Cyclists and motorists have equal ownership of the roads and few
bikes are ever stolen (although its always advisable to carry a lock). The ADFC
Fahrradstadtplan is available from most bike shops and gives a detailed plan of
cycle routes. Bikes can be rented from Fahrradstation (tel: 2045 4500;
www.fahrradstation.de).

EMERGENCY

If your property is stolen, contact the police immediately. The Central Police
Station is at Platz der Luftbrücke 6, Tempelhof (tel: 466 40). In case of emer-
gency call Police 110, Ambulance/Fire Brigade 112.

TAXIS

Taxis can be expensive – €2.50 before you start and €1.50 for every km. If travelling a short distance, ask for a *kurzstrecke* – this will take you 2km for a flat €3, but is only available on the street. Cabs can be ordered 24 hours a day from tel: 261 026.

TELEPHONES

To call Berlin from the UK, dial 00, then 49 for Germany and 30 for Berlin.

TIPPING

In resturants, service is usually added to the bill (see Eat) – look for the words *Bedienung Inclusiv*. Round taxi fares up to the nearest euro.

TOURIST INFORMATION

The Berlin Tourismus Marketing (BTM) operates three tourist offices (tel: 250 025; www.berlin-tourist-information.de). Branches can be found at Parisier Platz, Budapester Straße 45 and Alexanderplatz. Also check out Euraide (www.euraide.de) in the Zoo station.

TRAINS

Berlin has two train systems: the S-bahn (overground) and U-bahn (underground). Information on both can be found at www.bvg.de. Tickets for both can be purchased from yellow machines on station platforms. Weekly, day, single and short-distance (three U- or S-bahn stops and six on the bus or tram) tickets can be purchased. Be sure to validate your ticket after purchase. Officious inspectors regularly check the trains and will issue on-the-spot fines if you fail to produce a valid ticket. Bikes can be taken on the S-bahn and on the U-bahn during off-peak hours, although you must purchase an extra ticket.

Hg2 Berlin

index